TRANSCENDING *the* Color LINE

TRANSCENDING
C*the*olor LINE

The Sociology
of **BLACK EXPERIENCE**
in America

BOBBY E. MILLS, PhD

NEW YORK

TRANSCENDING *the* Color LINE
The Sociology of BLACK EXPERIENCE *in America*

Published in New York, New York, by Morgan James Publishing. Morgan James and The Entrepreneurial Publisher are trademarks of Morgan James, LLC. www.MorganJamesPublishing.com

The Morgan James Speakers Group can bring authors to your live event. For more information or to book an event visit The Morgan James Speakers Group at www.TheMorganJamesSpeakersGroup.com.

All Scripture is taken from the King James Version of the Holy Bible.

A **free** eBook edition is available
with the purchase of this print book.

CLEARLY PRINT YOUR NAME ABOVE IN UPPER CASE

Instructions to claim your free eBook edition:
1. Download the BitLit app for Android or iOS
2. Write your name in **UPPER CASE** on the line
3. Use the BitLit app to submit a photo
4. Download your eBook to any device

ISBN 978-1-63047-316-7 paperback
ISBN 978-1-63047-317-4 eBook
ISBN 978-1-63047-318-1 hardcover
Library of Congress Control Number:
2014944083

Cover Design by:
Rachel Lopez
www.r2cdesign.com

Interior Design by:
Bonnie Bushman
bonnie@caboodlegraphics.com

In an effort to support local communities, raise awareness and funds, Morgan James Publishing donates a percentage of all book sales for the life of each book to Habitat for Humanity Peninsula and Greater Williamsburg.

Get involved today, visit
www.MorganJamesBuilds.com

Habitat
for Humanity®
Peninsula and
Greater Williamsburg
Building Partner

TABLE OF CONTENTS

ACKNOWLEDGMENTS

The sociology of my personal experience has been grounded in meaningful, spiritually based, personal and professional life experiences and relationships. In the same way, the essays in this book are the product of loving family relationships—especially with my wife Larnita, son Daryl, and daughters Kelly and Karen—professional relationships, and personal longtime friendships.

Therefore, grateful appreciation and heartfelt thanks are extended to Clara M. Bowman for her assistance with the manuscript organization and formatting. To Denise Christine Brown, who read the manuscript for organizational structure and writing style. To Charles W. Moore, for our friendship and stimulating, spiritually based philosophical discussions over thirty-five years of attempting to make a difference in black community life as well as society in general. To Pastor Raymond L. Farley, for our spiritually based friendship over the past thirty-five years.

Finally, to Amanda Rooker at SplitSeed, for her tireless professional editing of the manuscript, as well as her spiritual insights in helping to bridge the racial divide in American society.

I love and thank you all; therefore, God bless you and yours!

INTRODUCTION

This collection of essays is a philosophical attempt at making sense out of the American black collective experience. These essays do not reflect traditional sociological theoretical perspectives and methodological considerations. Instead, the query is: How do we actually live? More importantly, what are we willing to sacrifice in order to live the way we say we want to live? Invariably the search for moral understanding and spiritual meaning is neither easy nor popular. It is indeed the abstract empirical (amoral and apolitical) character of sociology that has all but rendered it irrelevant to the resolution of contemporary social problems. In short, it is the biased initial theoretical assumptions of the scientific method (abstract empiricism) that are the social basis for collective bias via the illusion of value neutrality. This collective cultural bias is the social foundation for institutional racism, sexism, theological dogmatism (denominationalism), and above all authoritarianism. An "ism" is a schism, and schisms divide. Without a doubt, "either/or" logic fosters cultural extremism rather than a universal perspective on humanity.

So perhaps our true query is: should sociology be the sociology of social justification (democratic elitism) or the sociology of social justice (freedom and social equity)?

I offer this collection of essays as a down payment on the sociology of freedom. We need to heal the racial divide in American society once and for all. My hope is that these essays will serve as an intellectual framework for reconciling some of the numerous ideological contradictions that exist between individuals, ethnic social groups, and members of American society in general. They are all based on the understanding that the longest journey is the journey within, and it begins with the first steps of self-introspection. God hates prejudice and racism. The story of Moses's marriage to the Cushite woman teaches us this profound spiritual lesson. The anger of Aaron and Miriam because of the marriage of Moses caused God to descend from heaven in a pillar of cloud and stand at the doorway of the tent (see Numbers 1-16; God created all individuals out of one blood. Life and death are in the tongue, not skin color. "Keep your tongue from evil, and your lips from speaking guile" Psalm 34:13). God is an ever present help; however when God makes His presence known, He shows up and shows out for the righteousness of His kingdom and then moves on.

Within any social group, the task of a leader is threefold: to have a vision for the future (particularly for the children), to lead by visionary example, and to take followers where they have not been. Also, individuals cannot become good leaders unless they have been good followers. As an ethnic group, blacks have three basic primary institutions: family, church, and historically black colleges and universities (HBCUs). All three have major dysfunctional issues, and blacks must take responsibility for the existence of these institutional dysfunctions. (Blacks also have two secondary social institutions: barber shops and beauty salons.)

Unfortunately, all three primary institutions are in a state of moral and spiritual decline because the leadership in all three institutions has devolved into a self-serving mentality. Yet it is also true that blacks have lost a sense of tight-knit community, which came under attack by the forces of institutional racism during the process of desegregation. Therefore it is also my hope that this collection of essays will inspire some creative ideas about revitalizing our spiritual, moral, and socio-economic institutions as we attempt to recover the universal sense of common humanity lost in the desegregation process.

In my opinion, the cornerstone problem in the black community is the inability of blacks to hold each other accountable. One white man can hold one thousand blacks accountable, but one thousand blacks cannot hold one black individual accountable. As a result of institutional racism and the horrible after-effects of chattel slavery, whites have become the only ones who can discipline blacks. (Of course, this is not by choice but by institutional and cultural design.) Those who have the power to discipline through the strength of the law and the gun inherently have social and cultural rule. Yet increasingly it has also become virtually impossible for blacks to morally discipline each other because of the spiritual and moral decay of the institutional structures of the black community, namely the attitude that "nobody can tell me anything."

By and large, in the white community ideas rule. Intellectuals in the white community can ascend to the forefront of community development and therefore easily influence community affairs and institutional arrangements, because ideas make money. In other words, ideas rule, not money. This is how leadership roles in the white community are institutionalized (and universalized). In contrast, leadership roles in the black community tend to be personality driven, based on our "slave heritage." The black community then becomes a victim of one-dimensional "group think." Black intellectuals tend to be shunned and sometimes even ostracized. Almost everywhere in the black community, the open competition of ideas is discouraged and oftentimes stymied.

Specifically, leaders come primarily from the ranks of black pastors and black politicians, who themselves, as a whole, create conditions that divide the black community. On the one hand, black pastors talk about abstract faith apart from action. But "What doth it profit, my brethren, though a man say he hath faith, and have not works" (James 2:14)? Faith without works is dead, yet black pastors rarely talk about faith manifested as works of righteousness. On the other hand, black politicians deal with one-party politics (although for a profound reason) and oftentimes even the politics of race. One major political party uses the "lure" of openness, and the other major political party appears to operate with closed-door intentions toward minorities. This brings to mind Mark 8:36: "For what shall it profit a man, if he shall gain the whole world, and lose his own soul?" Therefore both sides are not always heard, understood, or even appreciated. If the black community is to become spiritually whole, intellectually productive, and above all morally integrated, these conditions must be altered radically.

The black community is victimized by a leadership mentality that is, to say the least, obsolete. This old guard leadership mentality cannot lead, it will not follow, and of course it will not voluntarily step aside. This social fact alone keeps the black community in a perpetual state of mental confusion, dysfunction, and moral chaos. In short, this old guard leadership mentality has led the black community into the wilderness of non-productivity and economic dependency. A "clarion call" is blowing across the land: change the guard or perish. When a people lack vision they will indeed perish, and the only lasting visions come from God.

Old worldviews are dying, and new worldviews are being born, laced with strange and new dimensions. New worldviews demand new thought processes and a different type of leadership mentality. The black community can no longer afford the luxury of political leaders who are cosmetic in their approach to power and authority, clergymen who are spiritual entertainers, and college administrators who are ebony tower elitists.

Finally, these essays are an earnest philosophical attempt to help blacks, as well as whites, learn to transcend the color line, because sin is the issue, not skin pigmentation. It is indeed unfortunate that one of the main problems in American society is still the color line. If America is to survive and thrive as a great nation, we must learn to live beyond the color line—that is, beyond the graveyard. While the black mindset tends to be a response to "white institutional and cultural racism,"the white mindset tends to focus on obtaining privileges without a sense of collective responsibility (i.e., public accountability). In other words, too many whites desire to be served, rather than to serve. This sense of self-imposed superiority on the part of white culture has created a play master psyche among many whites.

God is God because He knows how to serve. Yet at some level all humans still want privileges without collective social responsibility. The self-fulfilling prophecy of whites thinking and acting as though they are superior (or dominant) and blacks thinking and acting as though they are inferior is the main reason why whites and blacks cannot transcend the graveyard in their relationships with each other. As the prophet Ezekiel witnessed, only God can make dry bones live again (Ezekiel 37), because only God has resurrection power.

In light of all these realities, do we have a prayer of true reform and reconciliation? Yes, we do—although it might be all we have. Fortunately, it is all we need, because God plus the individual represent a moral majority. Put simply, prayer changes things institutional power cannot.

The "big game" is over. The life of Jesus provided a powerful spiritual lesson about human community, and He was taken out of the game of life by the children of men. Children of men tell "little white lies," but children of God tell the truth all the time. Social behavior is culturally and environmentally conditioned, not skin-color conditioned. There are some things that whites can learn from blacks about life, and likewise there are some things that blacks can learn from whites about life. Of course, there are some things that each group does that the other group should vehemently shun.

There is a spiritual war being waged in American society that is eating away at the most profound declaration in the history of humankind: "We hold these truths to be self-evident that all men are created equal and endowed with certain inalienable rights from their Creator...." Sad as it is, this spiritual war has led to ungodly discussions about the right to do wrong (self-centeredness), rather than the responsibility to do right. Indeed, the "me, myself, and I" syndrome has horrific social consequences.

We all know that America is no longer a racist society by law. The 1964 Civil Rights Act and the 1965 Voting Rights Act legally ended institutional racism in American society (despite the fact that the Supreme Court recently stripped the legislation of key enforcement provisions). However, institutional racism is still a central feature of American social life. Institutional racism must be viewed primarily as a "white problem"—that is, of whites' negative attitudes. Yet the external problem of institutional racism can only be fully eradicated when black people resolve their own internal problems, namely the lack of institutional cooperation and effectiveness of leadership. After all, cooperation is the definition of what delineates a social system.

As the following essays will argue, cooperation is best learned first in a family structure. Children must grow up seeing their mothers cooperating with their fathers, and likewise seeing their fathers loving their mothers. This combination provides the foundation for healthy personalities and positive values and character traits in young people.

Values determine the character of institutional structures, and institutional structures in turn determine the quality of life for individuals and social groups, job opportunities, and life advancement opportunities. By and large, black institutions are not capable of creatively dealing with a complex social structure that has been designed to dehumanize and exploit specific units in American society. Black institutions do not morally affirm the essential divine worth of blackness. Our quest then must be for harmonized unity. Our focus must not be on protesting in the streets, but rather on developing our minds and our analytical thinking skills. It is time for a "silent revolution"—blacks learning how to control their own thoughts.

The problem of social change is indeed perplexing because it involves changing human personalities and character traits in addition to external structures. The silent revolution has three concrete goals: (1) the creation of an internal spiritual value system, rather than an external materialistic value system, (2) the development of an egalitarian rather than authoritarian model of leadership, and (3) the restructuring of the family as a spiritual rather than an economic unit. Family is the basic foundational unit of society, because the capacity to live in society begins in the family. The family is "God's school for love"—where we learn both self-love and how to love and cooperate with others. This silent revolution can transform self as well as society without firing a single shot. What's needed is a renaissance of the human spirit.

So this collection of essays is primarily an attempt to hold the black community accountable from within. As a nation within a nation, blacks have lost sight of a national purpose. Free-thinking individuals are creative individuals who are enslaved by no force and are in unity with all. Dr. Martin Luther King Jr. wanted an individual to be able to ride the bus in dignity; our task is to first seek a dignified individual. This is not to say that Dr. King was not concerned with the kind of individual that sits on the bus; of course, he sought new behaviors. Yet we must seek more than just new behaviors; we must seek to become new beings. Not to know is bad, but not to want to know is even worse. Not to aspire is unthinkable. And not to hope is unforgivable.

For the generations not yet born, it is imperative that we keep hope alive. The opportunity has come in this present moment. What shall we do with it? It is roll-call time; the clarion call has been sounded! Arise, black people of America, and claim the spiritual heritage of your forefathers, never to walk in darkness again! Because once a social group loses knowledge of "self" it is impossible to integrate with the oppressor. This is why we have only had desegregation, not integration. The truth is a map for eternity. Therefore, no more rapping. Let's start mapping.

1 THE SOCIOLOGY OF FAMILY: SPIRITUALITY VERSUS MATERIALISM

Increasing rates of family disorganization (i.e., any deviation from two-parent families including the biological mother and father) is highly correlated with the development of twentieth-century urban ghettos, urbanization in general, secularization, and the information technology explosion. Combine these social factors with the moral decline of American society in general, and what we have is an underclass not of illegitimate children but illegitimate parents. By illegitimate parents, I mean individuals who were together for pleasure and not out of godly love for each other.

This does not in any way excuse the impact of institutional racism on the family structure and family life of blacks. The economic structure of American society has forced families in general to function solely based on economic terms rather than as a non-contractual commitment based on unconditional love. Therefore, poor individuals have more stresses and strains on their relationships than middle- and upper-class families. Paying the cost to be the boss in poor families is a real issue.

To be sure, there is a social correlation between family economics and family structure. A large percentage of the disorganization in black family structure is related to a lack of family income, because job opportunities and economics determine the lifestyle and the institutional structure of a social group. However, having a two-parent family is not an insurance policy against material poverty, particularly if you are a member of a minority group. Mexican-Americans have had traditionally low rates of family disorganization, yet their overall rate of economic poverty equals that found in the black community. In short, the disorganization in black family structure is not merely due to institutional racism or poverty alone. The inability of black men to provide for family survival needs causes additional internal family tensions and interpersonal conflicts.

Yet the intent here is to describe the purpose of family life in objective spiritual terms, not to moralize about social pathology. Viewed through an objective spiritual lens, black family structures mirror white family structures. The objective is not to blame the victim but rather to take a hard-nosed look at the nature of institutional structures and culture in general. The economic structure of American society is increasingly more caste-like in character. The concept of social mobility is becoming an excuse for inequality, as money remains relatively fixed at the top. Therefore, given the external adversity under which blacks are forced to function individually and collectively, what should astound us is not the rate of family dissolution but the fact that any families stay intact at all.

The family is the basic social unit of every society. It is indeed *the* significant socializer. The family is the basis for personality and character development. Individuals can have family happiness if and only if they are willing to pay the cost. One never really gets something for nothing— life isn't that simple. For, after all, nothing from nothing invariably leaves nothing. It is for this reason alone that Jesus always urged individuals to anticipate the spiritual and social cost of everything they do.

Family ought to be based on a love association that occurs *before* marriage rather than after. This is important because there are many individuals who are married but do not really like one another. I say "like" because like must come before love. Love is an all-encompassing concept that requires total commitment. Unfortunately, marriage for most Americans (not just blacks) is an economic arrangement rather than a lifelong commitment based on unconditional love. Capitalism fosters the development of a "rugged individualistic" approach to family life in that it forces individual members of a family to function as individuals rather than as a spiritual association.

Happiness and self-fulfillment are supposed to be experienced within the context of family life. The notion of rugged individualism as a social fact explains the virtual nonexistence of the extended family structure in American society. The competition for material things is so fierce that it forces individuals to psychically live alone. To be sure, the divorce rate, family size, abortion, retirement homes, and child abuse are all directly related to the economic system and the value orientation that undergirds our collective materialistic mentality. An economic system that engenders materialism as a way of life destroys the basis of society, family, and the valuation of the sanctity of life.

THE QUALITIES OF A SPIRITUAL FAMILY

- A spiritual family must be based on *friendship*, which combines temperamental compatibility, sympathetic understanding, mutual confidence, and high moral ideals.
- A spiritual family assumes equality of responsibility and a spirit of democracy in reaching family decisions.
- A spiritual family stresses the significance of spiritual living for the development of human personality and/or character.

- A spiritual family recognizes personal happiness as an objective to be secured through family life.
- A spiritual family stresses the principle of loving, sacrificing, and giving, never expecting anything in return.
- A spiritual family positions the Spirit of God at the center of family life: at the marriage altar, when the new house is built, when the baby comes, when hard times come.

The church is God's house of prayer, and it is here that the meaning of family life ought to be illuminated and spiritually strengthened. In other words, finding creative ways to make family life religious is a *collective societal responsibility*, and local churches should view it as their responsibility to help strengthen families one by one.[1]

---

1   For more on this topic, see Bobby E. Mills, *Let the Church Be the Church* (Morgan James, 2014).

2 CHARACTER DEVELOPMENT: MAKING YOU YOUR BEST FRIEND

The human mind is God's most precious gift to individuals. Indeed, it is very delicate and even fragile. Human free will is also a precious gift from God. Lack of motivation, inadequate discipline, and the absence of personal integrity can do to one's mind what lack of exercise and improper eating habits can do to one's physical health. Making life an ongoing learning experience is largely a matter of developing the right mindset. Therefore, if an individual is not consciously developing this kind of positive mindset, he may well be creating a formidable foe: himself. An individual's mind is his best defense against dehumanization and exploitation either of self or other.

Without a doubt, character development is about spiritual and internal values rather than material and external values. An external value system invariably undermines the humanity and divinity of individuals.

Indeed, individuals do not live by physical bread alone. An external value system institutionalizes matter over mind. Elevating matter over mind creates an unnatural state of human existence. Positing the physical/ material world as more important than the spiritual world invariably creates *anomie* (meaninglessness, self-estrangement, isolationism, powerlessness, and normlessness). It is not skin color and culture that make a man a man but moral character.

In valuing only material things, individuals deny the spiritual basis of their existence. Therefore, rather than participating in "being," they participate in non-being (meaninglessness). Material objects are unconscious and have no meaning in and of themselves. Unfortunately, individuals decide that material goodies mean everything and self is nothing; therefore, human life comes cheaply. This in turn erodes the basis for human-centered living (community). However, community is unquestionably the presupposed context of human existence. In other words, we express our humanity/ divinity through the material world rather than keep it inside of us.

Reality is determined by our self-consciousness, which is the mind reflecting about itself. (Our self-consciousness in turn is determined by our values.) I think; therefore, I am what I think. I am that I am, and what I am I give to all. Thus, the art of understanding (thinking) is a necessary condition for human-centered living. The material world is only a part of reality. It is not reality itself.

The prophet Ezekiel puts it this way: "One day I was walking, and way up in the middle of the air I saw a big wheel [the physical world]. But I did not stop looking once I saw the big wheel, because outward appearance is not always inward reality. So I looked again! This time I saw a wheel in a wheel, and there were interlocking wheels. At the center of all the wheels was a little wheel [the spiritual world], and it was turning all the other wheels. In other words, I saw the whole thing [reality], and the little wheel was indeed the big wheel, and the big wheel was nothing without the little wheel. The little wheel was the servant" (Ezekiel 1:15-27, author's paraphrase).

An external value system creates negativism and violence. An external value system forces individuals into examining others rather than themselves. If individuals are focused on the attributes of others, they will likely conclude that they themselves are more deserving than others. Why? If one focuses on the attributes of others, he will notice that they don't do anything to help him; in fact, they don't do anything to help themselves--so why should he care about what happens to them? As a result, selfish hoarding becomes the principle of life rather than generous sharing.

On the other hand, if one thinks about self first, he will come to know himself (his own strengths and weaknesses). More importantly, an individual will learn how to view others more positively and therefore be generous. That is, an individual will learn how to give his most precious possession—himself—to others. If one knows self, then one cannot be false to anyone. When an individual changes the way he views the world, he has changed the world. In fact, the only world you have is your world, because an individual can only control his own mind (thoughts). An individual cannot know himself by focusing his perception on others.

Therefore, external values engender the institutionalization of negativism toward others and invariably foster human exploitation. Searching for meaning on the outside (external values) ultimately results in meaninglessness, because meaning cannot be found externally. Moreover, human exploitation is an act void of meaning, and a social system based on exploitation results in institutionalized suicide—the ultimate expression of meaninglessness. Thus, in American society we have created an environment that is void of meaning and national purpose. This problem of meaninglessness raises two questions: (1) How do we live? (2) What are we willing to give up to live the way we say we want to live?

Without a doubt, there is no external institutional structure in American society that generates internal spiritual values. The Christian church has failed miserably socio-politically, socio-spiritually, and in terms of community development. As they say, eleven o'clock on Sunday mornings is the most racially and ethnically segregated hour in our society. The Christian church's socio-political foundation (denominationalism) has not been able to effectively enhance social democracy in American society. Instead, the church has been the main culprit in the institutionalization of authoritarianism (individualism)—without understanding that authoritarianism is the foundation of all of the evil schisms (lies) that alienate individuals from each other and indeed from God (communism, fascism, racism, sexism, and so on).

The oneness of humanity means social-cost accountability, not individualism, racialism, sexism, or any other "ism." Institutional racism clearly depicts the need for collective character and integrity. For example, on a one-to-one basis, a person can find individual whites who seemingly possess positive character traits, but God forbid if two or more whites come around; then the "manure" hits the fan.

To be sure, individuals are socially classified into various economic, religious, racial/ethnic, and political groupings. These external reference groups are powerful social factors in the development of our internal self-identities. They are also powerful factors in our cultural socialization and the development of our value orientations (lifestyles). In fact, practically speaking, these external reference groups take precedence over our internal self-identities. Reference groups reflect who individuals are and what they want to become. That is, the reference group is the looking-glass self. This also means that the group is the power source, and the individual is effectively powerless in his ability either to influence or alter the group's image.

Since the group is the power source, if one seeks to influence the group's image in a positive manner, he faces socio-political ostracism and possibly physical death. That is, an individual becomes cut off from what may be perceived to have ultimate value (material goodies), but more importantly is cut off from a sense of self as defined by the reference group. Selfhood then is lost in a mirage of meaninglessness. Self-estrangement produces symptoms of schizophrenic paranoia. If one's reference group is void of meaning (in the form of positive character traits,) an individual invariably learns to dislike self. Reference group anomie produces individual anomie.

Under the present social system, positive group self-esteem is virtually impossible, and positive individual self-esteem is nonexistent. Why? First, individuals dislike the reference groups to which they belong. Whites dislike the external identity of "whiteness" and therefore seek to establish a positive sense of self-worth—typically within their own ethnic group. This social fact alone explains the saliency of ethnicity in American society over and above social democracy (i.e., the melting-pot theory). Yet if the universal social identity is meaningless, then the particular ethnic identity is meaningless. Unfortunately, individuals, regardless of color, tend to find it difficult to live in a community of equals without creating social stratification.

This social fact is equally true of the "permanently tan" ethnic groups in America. Blacks have been socialized into disliking the external identity of "blackness," Hispanics the external identity of "Hispanicness," and so on. The saliency of race and class in American society has in turn produced a governmental system based wholly on interest group politics (protectionism), rather than equality of opportunity. Put simply, this is the politics of Armageddon. This is why there is just as much exploitation (meaninglessness) in one own's ethnic group as there is in larger society.

Within this kind of political system, money becomes the (false) god and the medium of exploitation (rooted in greed, envy, and jealousy). All individuals then prostitute themselves to varying degrees to obtain money. Individual whites accommodate themselves to the insanity of racism because it means a "better" job, and a better job means more money. The more money one has to spend, the more material goodies he can obtain—and the worth of an individual in American society is determined by material possessions. Ethnic minorities in American society prostitute themselves to whites in order to "hold off" the ever-constant threat of physical and symbolic death that whites represent. Therefore, in American society there is no such animal as the justice of money—only the use of people for money.

Like death, exploitation is the great equalizer. It does not respect artificial and arbitrary differences in status. Not only do all of us die physically, but unfortunately the overwhelming majority of us also die spiritually through exploitation, becoming lifetime card-carrying members of the "walking dead" club. We may have no choice regarding physical death, but we do have a choice regarding spiritual death.

In the book of Samuel, there are two versions of an episode of conflict between Saul and David. Saul was king of Israel, the divinely appointed leader of the Israelites. He was appointed to be the champion of religion, and he considered David to be a troublemaker. Yet the book of Samuel tells us that the content of David's character was nobler and more winsome than that of the chief official of institutional religion. Why? The answer is simple: because David had suffered from the unwarranted persecution of Saul. Saul had been hunting David to kill him. David could have killed Saul, but he rose above the religious code of his day, which was "an eye for an eye and a tooth for a tooth."

In other words, David had a conscience. He possessed genuine religious character. David lived his religion. When Saul finally met David face to face, he saw himself for what he really was and broke down. He lifted up his voice and wept, "Thou art more righteous than I, for thou hast rewarded me good, whereas I have rewarded thee evil" (1 Samuel 24:17). Great is the individual who rules his own spirit (mind). He who rules his own spirit is greater than he who takes a city. David was a member of God's spiritual kingdom. The lesson is clear: the weak invariably exploit the weak. The strong take the giant step of overcoming evil (negativism) with good (positivism, or charitable service).

This leads us to the following question: what has institutional religion done to our characters? One can believe the Christian Bible from cover to cover but still remain uninspired by God's truth. The truth is that equal is equal, not "more or less" equal. In the same way, one may believe many things about Jesus but still remain uninspired by His teachings or life. None of us is born with a fully developed character. Nor does our character form spontaneously on its own. Character development is a long process, and only Christ-centered Christianity can develop it.

Institutional Christianity has failed to produce high moral character because we have made it into individualism, racism, sexism, status differentiation, and above all a process of economic exploitation. If our external selves and our internal selves are not perfect matches, society becomes a Pandora's Box, a ball of confusion. We need the moral integration of flesh and spirit. In the same way, positive character traits must exist on both the collective and individual levels. For character development requires a creative tension between the spiritual and material worlds.

Jesus lifted up the concept of man and gave us a positive image of selfhood. Character cannot be taught like scientific facts. It must be inspired by example and positive behavior modeling. Whenever we set the scene properly, the Spirit of God that was in Jesus always comes back, sometimes in the lives of men like Martin Luther King Jr., John F. Kennedy, Malcolm X, President Jimmy Carter, and so on.

Like Pilate, we tend to wash our hands in despair, call it quits, and say let the record stand. Yes, we may always have poverty, violence, and social injustice, because there will always be people who are not willing to set positive examples of character for others to imitate. Children of men "play" outside (according to external values), but children of God live on the inside (according to internal values). Indeed, children of men remain children forever because they tell little white lies. The children of God always speak the truth in *love*. Hence, an individual should not prostitute himself to any human being or material thing, but only to God, because God has no material needs. Institutional religion should be about moral and spiritual character development.

Doubt rule yourself, be tolerant.
—Hegel

3 THE PROPER USE OF MONEY

Wealth can be a cruel master, even as cruel a master as one's worst adversary, the devil. "No one can serve two masters: for either he will hate the one and love the other, or he will hold to one and despise the other. You cannot serve God and mammon" (Matthew 6:24). The Bible declares that King Solomon was the wisest man to have ever lived because he asked God for wisdom, not money. However, God gave him enormous wealth because he asked for the right thing: "But seek ye first the Kingdom of God, and His righteousness; and all these things shall be added unto you" (Matthew 6:33). God has said what he will provide if you seek first the Kingdom of God: food, clothing, and shelter. "All scripture is given by inspiration of God, and is profitable for doctrine, for reproof, for correction, for instruction in righteousness: That the man of God may be perfect, thoroughly furnished unto all good works" (2 Timothy 3:16–17).

The Bible declares that it is easier for a camel to go through the eye of a needle than it is for a rich man to go to heaven (Matthew 19:24). The question is, why? The answer lies in humankind's inability to control their greed, pursuit of fleshy pleasure, and exercise power and influence properly without attempting to "play God." It has been profoundly stated that "to whom much is given, much is required." Unfortunately, rich individuals often do not understand this social fact, because their desire is to accumulate more and more wealth.

The story of the rich barn builder is an appropriate analogy. "And he said, This will I do: I will pull down my barns, and build greater; and there will I bestow all my fruits and my goods. And I will say to my soul, thou hast much goods laid up for many years; take thine ease, eat, drink, and be merry. But God said unto him, Thou fool, this night thy soul shall be required of thee: then whose shall those things be, which thou hast provided?" (Luke 12:18–20). The moral of the story is this: "Do all the good you can, while you can, and when you can, for as many as you can." God's desire is that we love and serve each other, not exploit each with wealth, understanding, and knowledge. For after all, righteousness and goodness are the greatest forces in the world.

In the black community, the economic business structure is primarily based upon the unbridled construction of night clubs and religious church houses—in other words, on nighttime fantasies and daytime illusions. (Chapter 12 will discuss this economic focus on "Saturday night and Sunday morning" in more detail.) It is indeed unfortunate that too many religious leaders use the enterprise of religion (church houses) as their personal banks, fueling the flame of unbridled religious competition, or "My religious enterprise (kingdom) is greater than yours." This ungodly process stifles creative economic development in the black community, which could be used to develop credit unions, banks, hotels/motels, drug stores, gas stations, and so on.

Too many religious leaders become consumers and economic slaves of the superficial status symbols of wealth: expensive cars, expensive clothing, expensive jewelry, multi-million dollar homes, and helicopters/airplanes—and above all, they spoil their children with things. The "bling-bling" so-called "reality" television show *Preachers of LA* is a classic vulgar example of this unbridled religious shakedown. Sociologically, this conspicuous consumption indicates a desire to be seen rather than heard, because one has nothing meaningfully productive to say to others. After all, true wealth would be *owning* the corporations that produce these status-symbol goodies. Consumption is just consumption, and fuels the wealth of others.

Becoming spiritually fruitful, multiplying, and being a good steward is what life is all about. Yet in most unbridled religious organizations, there is no itemized annual budget for parishioners to inspect, examine, and hold religious leaders accountable to for creatively utilizing resources for community development.

When used properly, individuals can use money as a tool to create economic independence for themselves as well as their families. That is, money is only a means to an end, not an end in and of itself. When used improperly, rather than a tool, money becomes a *fool* individuals use to create economic slavery for themselves and their families, and they end up with nothing at all. Unfortunately, the latter is the case in too many instances. As it has been profoundly said, "A fool and his money will soon part ways."

RULES FOR BORROWING MONEY

1. Don't borrow money. Be a lender rather than a borrower.
2. If you must borrow money, borrow money from your family and friends, because they will probably forgive you if you do

not pay them back. Banks and other lending institutions do not have a forgiving spirit.

3. Always partner and become friends with someone who has money. Typically, minority individuals spend a lot of money rather than save a lot of money.

4. Know the difference between expenses and investments/assets. Cars and clothes are expenses, not investments/assets. Therefore, forget the bling-bling show and save the *dough*.

Money is not God, and God is not attempting to save money. God is God all by himself. Money is simply a man-made instrument for the exchanging and purchasing of goods and services in the marketplace. God requires that we become good stewards of money. To paraphrase King Solomon (see Proverbs 4): Money is good as a defense. Knowledge is good as a defense. But the excellency of wisdom is to acquire a good understanding, and a good understanding is based upon spirituality (God)—that is, common sense. Pray for wisdom (common sense) and it will be granted.

Unfortunately, common sense is not common. God has said through his servant King David, "I have been young, and now I am old; yet have I not seen the righteous forsaken, nor his seed begging bread" (Psalm 37:25). The righteous live by faith. Too many Americans do not look back historically or reach back behind them to help others, which would create a future that includes rather than excludes. So be it.

4 ONE EDUCATIONAL PROCESS DOES NOT FIT ALL

P ublic schooling of the masses is one of the cornerstones of American democracy. Multiculturalism is another. However, multiculturalism in public schooling has failed to produce the melting pot our society has idealized. Instead, we simply have another situation of "separate but equal" (that is, unequal). The truth is that public school systems are better at educating certain cultural groups and social classes than others, and too many urban children are falling through the public school cracks. In this case, it's not the children who are failing but the schools that are failing the children. To solve this problem, we need to incorporate a system of self-paced learning in the public schools to account for cultural differences. In the meantime, we also need an immediate process to rescue those children that the public school system is currently failing.

In a multicultural society, the educational process should be based upon individualization, not centralization. Primary and elementary school curricula should reflect the cultural-ethnic differences that are expressed in economic inequalities, family structure differences, parenting skill differences, values orientations, and learning style differences. On the other hand, high school curricula should reflect the dominant middle-class cultural values of "how to get ahead in a technology-based, information-oriented society." Middle-class values are not really about making money but about self-development; nothing reflects middle-class values better than obtaining a quality education.

We live in a fatherless society, especially in the black community. Unfortunately, public schooling has not adjusted its structure to accommodate the needs of children who come from one-parent families. All children have biological fathers, but few have spiritual "daddies" in the home. This social fact alone adversely affects the nature of public schooling. In order to be effective, public schooling must function as a surrogate family structure. Without a doubt, the teaching and training of children in matters of behavioral manners is the responsibility of parents. Unfortunately, many children enter the public schooling process undisciplined and without the emotional intelligence to be able to sit in a structured classroom environment and behave appropriately.

To a large degree, all education is about moral education and character development. In ethnic communities, religion plays an important role in communal life. Therefore, public schooling should reflect a sense of moral order (internalized self-discipline) and sacredness, not just profaneness. Most teachers spend approximately 80 percent of their time seeking to maintain classroom order (decorum) without the management tool of corrective discipline. When families fail to teach behavioral manners and emotional intelligence, the responsibility then shifts to the public schooling process. Society cannot expect teachers to maintain classroom order without giving them the management tool of corrective discipline. In current public schooling systems, both teachers and students are frustrated. Schools employ policemen to stand guard to maintain superficial order, rather than facilitate an environment where moral internal order can be maintained.

In the public schooling process, all things must work together for the good of those who love children, because children are our future and thus our immortality. Administrators, teachers, and support staff must foster love, dedication, and service as the foundation of public schooling. Public schooling must not simply become a paycheck system. If so, then our nation is doomed. Public schooling must be based upon the philosophy of "children first," and of course, if children are first then we will "leave no child behind." Also, "no child left behind" is only half of the equation. "No parent left behind" completes the equation. Public schools must begin to provide parenting skills classes in the evenings for single-parent families.

Middle-class and upper-class children are taught before they are given standardized tests. Poor and working-class children are rarely if ever taught, but they are always given standardized tests. The ability to read and comprehend is the basis for performing adequately on standardized tests, as well as overall educational success, yet most poor and working-class children cannot read. The same is true for minority students: minority students are primarily failing state and national standardized tests because they cannot read. Because minority students are not taught adequate behavioral standards at home, teachers typically have to contend with too many disciplinary issues in the classroom to be able to teach reading effectively.

Of course, state and national tests are important evaluation tools that reflect middle-class values. Many minority students are not acquainted with middle-class value constructs, and therefore they do not understand how important social conduct (social behavior) is in relationship to successfully completing high school and becoming a productive citizen. This is why parental involvement in the educational development of their children must be factored into the overall grading system for student development.

The best example of a public school system creatively responding to the issue of school choice is the District of Columbia Public Schools in Washington, DC. In 1981, voters in DC considered a ballot initiative to bring widespread school choice to the District. The initiative was defeated by a nine-to-one margin. In the twenty-eight years since that vote, as many as fifty thousand students have dropped out of the DC public schools.

DC parents are beginning to give school choice a second look, and as a result sweeping reforms are occurring throughout District public schools. Based on the most recent national statistics (2011), DC has ninety-seven charter schools, enrolling approximately twenty-seven thousand students.[2] In addition, over two thousand students attend private schools using vouchers through the federally funded DC Opportunity Scholarship Program. It seems as though competition in a private enterprise system improves product quality even in education.

To be sure, the time has come for ethnic communities to seriously engage in a dialogue concerning the issue of school choice as a means of improving education quality. Providing a quality education for all Americans is the civil rights issue of the twenty-first century.

---

2 Charter School Enrollment (2013), National Center for Education Statistics, http://nces. ed.gov/programs/coe/indicator_cgb.asp.

5 THE MISEDUCATION OF THE BLACK COMMUNITY

The miseducation of the black community is at the crux of its collective nonproductivity. Educational systems are the primary vehicles for instilling consciousness in individuals. Unfortunately, educational systems in the black community reflect a commitment to standards and values that do not affirm the essential humanity and divinity of blackness. God willed all human beings to look the way He wanted them to look. Therefore, both blackness and whiteness are expressions of the will of God, and of course the will of God is that we "love one another."

Educational systems, built upon middle-class values, consciously and unconsciously insist that blacks take on self-rejection attitudes as part of a mentality that perpetuates white supremacy and black cultural oppression and marginalization. The consequence is the "Uncle Tom" syndrome. This social fact alone has kept the black community "behind the eight ball" and out in left field.

To be sure, the time has come for blacks to mentally emancipate themselves. Blacks must stop playing plantation games; they do not understand the rules or the game because they did not create either. Slavery must be understood as a physical, economic condition, not a mental state of being. After all, whites are not going to hold black leadership or institutions accountable to the working-class poor (i.e., the larger black community). This is something only blacks can do. Without a doubt, no one will save us from ourselves but us.

Herein is the crux of our educational dilemma: the so-called middle-class blacks have betrayed the black masses. That is, middle-class blacks are more concerned about protecting an individualistic materialistic lifestyle without understanding what truly defines the middle class. Values define the middle class, not money. There are numerous individuals in our society who have middle-class and even upper-class money, but they do not have middle-class and upper-class values.

Institutions mirror what individuals believe is most important in life as they determine quality of life and employment opportunities for individuals. Therefore, blacks must redefine their institutions in order to redefine themselves. The universal impact of free minds affects us all. Restructuring intellectual thought processes in the black community must be our first priority. Whites abolished chattel slavery because chattel slavery destroys initiative and incentive. No group of individuals will work and produce goods and services for others to the same extent they will for themselves. Whites clearly understood this social fact and therefore replaced chattel slavery with the idea of the sharecropper, a more sophisticated mechanism of social control. It goes without saying that sharecroppers never received their fair share of the crops they produced.

In particular, restructuring educational institutions in the black community is imperative. The time has come for the black community to take a hardnosed approach to the systems that rock the cradle of education for our community, namely our public schools. Educational institutions are our future, but our future is debased by a leadership mentality that does not know where it is headed. Educational leadership in the black community has an elitist rap but not an egalitarian map. Again, the social condition of the black experience needs a community of equals, not those who are "more or less" equal.

The educational system in the black community must create a community of equals. If black colleges are the head of the educational system, and the head is confused, then what about the body? Community development is fueled by creative ideas, and black colleges by and large are producing no such ideas regarding community development. Black colleges are in a state of confusion because they have sought to separate knowledge and understanding from moral values and spiritual principles. Moreover, educational methods in black colleges do not reflect the social realities of the larger community and therefore cannot promote a higher quality of life. But more importantly, as social institutions, black colleges do not serve as interdependent catalysts that reinforce or help to build other viable institutions in the black community.

As for me, I believe that three things must take place in order to halt the miseducation of blacks and above all integrate black colleges and universities with the larger community:

1. **The creation of community advisory boards made up of a cross-section of the black community.** Boards of trustees and regents function solely as political bodies in relationship to state funding sources, and therefore there is no direct input from the larger community into the internal operations of black colleges and universities. Since there is no direct input, there is little

or no direct output (in the form of social-cost accountability). To be sure, community advisory boards would be instrumental in the drive toward consistency between the internal self and external self.

2. **The development of community service wings in our colleges and universities.** A principal mission of historically black colleges and universities (HBCUs) ought to be to orient themselves to assessing community needs and problems, and therefore assist in resolving these on a reasonable basis.

3. **The restructuring of academic programs in order to reflect the social realities of the larger community.**

The proper function of an individual is to live creatively, not merely exist. Black colleges have been teaching blacks how to exist—merely how to make a living rather than how to live. This, of course, is why I have undertaken the fight to free our minds in order that our hind parts might follow. The black community surely needs intellectual warriors. Our fight is against those forces that militate against individuals controlling their own minds, and for the moral integration of humankind. In order to change, one must deny the self of today in order to pursue the unknown self of tomorrow. To change is to die. Strange and great are those who consciously "kill" themselves that they might live. Whites brought one particular economic structure to America. Blacks have created their own unique economic structure of stealing from one another. Black colleges must reaffirm that the basis for education is moral education.

6 WHAT HAPPENED TO THE WAR ON POVERTY?

ny racial or ethnic group that stands still will be washed away by the ideas of social change. Blacks have been standing still far too long. Institutions in the black community must again become centers for intellectual ferment, new ideas, and creative social changes. The time has come, but the question is, are blacks ready? It is time for the black community to cross over to newness of life, never to walk in spiritual darkness again.

Too many blacks do not fully comprehend the socio-political meaning of the resurgence of Republicanism. For over two decades, there was a steady movement toward reducing both the size and scope of the role of government—especially the federal government—because President Lyndon Johnson's War on Poverty program was assisting many black families to exit from the ranks of the underclass.

President Ronald Reagan's victory crowned the movement to reduce the size of the federal government, but its roots extended back to 1964 (i.e., the Goldwater era).

The New Deal coalition is no longer broad enough to elect a president or command congressional majorities. Roosevelt's New Deal was no deal at all for blacks. President Johnson's War on Poverty programs were targeted at the poor as compensation for past discrimination, rather than as a process to create equality of opportunity. Although these programs sought to create equality of outcome, instead they created stagflation and drained the resources and compassion of majority taxpayers.

To be sure, President Johnson was a compassionate and well-intentioned politician who wanted to resolve the problem of poverty in American society, and possibly institutional racism as well. The black community owes President Johnson their deepest respect. However, the bureaucrats were not so well intentioned; they took the money and ran, and the poor were left holding the poverty bag. Unfortunately, in the seventies, money was projected as the solution to poverty, rather than the clarification of values and character development.

Spiritually minded individuals know that you cannot buy your way out of poverty. The formula for getting out of poverty is called "thinking and working your way out." The War on Poverty programs empowered the government, not individuals. Jesus empowered individuals to rule over their own spirits.

To be sure, most Democratic politicians empower the government and themselves. Jesus illustrates this point in His story about the man at the pool at Bethesda (John 5). Jesus empowered this man to get up and move forward after thirty-eight years of mental immobility and non-productivity. Jesus did not further enslave the man, nor did He enslave the man to Himself. Rather, Jesus freed the man internally so that he could take full responsibility for his own social/biological condition. After all, Jesus did not put the man in the pool, and the man had been receiving some physical assistance during his thirty-eight years of non-productivity. The moral of the story is this: physical help alone does not resolve the issues associated with poverty. The resolution of poverty requires a spiritual empowerment.

"Reaganomics" was an enemy, but it was not *the* enemy. The lack of institutional and spiritual unity among blacks is the root cause of our institutional social disorganization. The black leadership mindset is too self-centered as well as self-serving. The structure of American society is based on the creative tension between individual initiatives and human interdependence, not self-centered individualism.

Blacks need to redefine their politics in order to secure a productive future for their children. The system should be neutral, neither Democratic nor Republican, and neither black nor white. Of course, there are those who for selfish reasons seek to make the system partisan. A system is simply based upon individuals cooperating with one another. And as established in an earlier essay, cooperation is best exampled within a family context. In the twenty-first century, too many black children grow up experiencing family conflict rather than family cooperation. Because cooperation is learned within the context of family, for good or evil, whites tend to cooperate with other whites.

The real issue is not party identity but individual and collective responsibility. God commanded that individuals work. Work is not a curse; it is the gift of God. Therefore, individuals must work for freedom, because no individual can give another individual something that is basically spiritual in nature (which freedom is). Real freedom is freedom of the human spirit and mind. The Democratic Party is not the solution, and the Republican Party is not the problem. Indeed, far too many blacks believe that the Democratic Party is the solution to all of their social problems. All individuals want freedom of choice, but few want the responsibility of accountability.

Traditionally, the philosophy of Republicanism was based upon responsibility, credibility, reliability, and accountability. In the twenty-first century, the Republican philosophy is not so clear. Nevertheless, most individuals want to debate issues of rights and privileges (such as abortion rights and homosexuality/same-sex marriage rights), not responsibilities and obligations.

America has spent over six trillion dollars on the War on Poverty. Unfortunately, the percentage of individuals who are poor is a little higher in 2013 than it was in 1965. The question is why. The War on Poverty failed because the majority of its programs were misguided— that is, most did not require character development and self-sufficiency. For now, faith-based initiatives might represent a more promising approach for effective governmental social assistance to those who are materially poor.

7

BLACK PERSONALITY STRUCTURE: AN EXPRESSION OF RACIAL OPPRESSION

The history of blacks in America is indeed the history of a group of people forced to view themselves through the eyes of others. Historically then blacks have been denied the basic human right of self-definition. In view of this social fact, it seems clear that racial oppression has produced a distinctive black personality—not in formal psychological terms, but in terms of cultural expression.

The human mind cannot be understood solely from the conscious psychological data that it produces. Indeed, the human mind is a complex apparatus for cultural adaptation; it facilitates the cultural adjustment of individuals to real-world hierarchies and to each other. Therefore, the mind serves as a mediator between individual internal needs and external social realities. Its function is to ensure the positive survival of the individual in his cultural environment. After all, an individual's mind is his or her only defense against dehumanization and exploitation, either from self or other. Thus, the art of understanding (thinking) is the unquestioned basis for human-centered community living.

"Individuals who live under the same institutional and environmental conditions have a certain similarity in their mental and emotional processes called basic personality structure. The basic personality structure of an individual is acquired through progressive integration during the whole life cycle; but with special emphasis on childhood."[3] The study of a group like African Americans presents this type of socio-psychology in a unique cultural context. The culture in which blacks function is American. Therefore, on the one hand, given the slave heritage of America, there are socio-cultural conditions that exist for blacks that do not exist for whites, and for the sake of brevity I shall call these social conditions "socio-cultural dehumanization." This socio-cultural force requires that blacks live within the confines of a caste-like cultural social system, which in turn seriously interferes with all varieties of creative cultural expression. Racial oppression then has a permanently negative impact on the black mindset and personality structure. The distinctive group experiences of blacks in America are therefore the root cause of the inability of blacks to positively legitimize their own existence—i.e., deeply and positively affirm the value of their selfhood.

James Baldwin, in his essay collection *Nobody Knows My Name*, states the problem precisely: "In America, the color of my skin had stood between me and myself. I left America because I had doubted my ability to survive the fury of the color problem. I wanted to find in what way this specialness could be made to connect me with other people instead of dividing me from them."[4] W. E. Dubois articulated

---

3   Abram Kardiner, *The Individual and His Society* (Columbia University Press, 1939), p. 335.
4   James Baldwin, *Nobody Knows My Name* (New York: Dial Press, 1961), p. 4.

the same notion when he asserted: "The Negro ever feels his twoness, an American and a Negro."[5] Thus everything that blacks possess and do not possess is an expression of racial oppression. That is, whites designed so-called democratic institutions for themselves and racial oppression as an institution for blacks.

Therefore, the most consistent feature of the black personality is that of organizing one's behavior around the main problem of white cultural adaptation—i.e., not offending whites. Racism is viewed as the central problem in the black community, mainly because of racial isolationism. Hence, the cultural adaptation of blacks is oriented toward the racial oppression they experience. To put it another way, one might say that black self-esteem is conditioned by the unpleasant images of self that constantly come from the behavior of whites toward blacks. There is no doubt then that there are constant pushes and pulls that are placed on individual blacks to balance white negative social expectations and positive internal self-image in order to protect the self from being disordered or destroyed. Obviously, this is a complex phenomenon, and any attempts at characterizing the expressions of an individual's personality as a group expression may border on falsity.

Nonetheless, the social fact of an externally imposed, distinctive group identity for blacks does exist. The question is whether this common group identity produces a distinctive personality structure. It is my belief that the black personality structure is a caricature of the corresponding white personality structure. There is no doubt that this leads to sameness in attitudinal motivation, which in part accounts for why some blacks in general do not deal with themselves positively. In view of this, it seems quite clear that there are few places in American society where a black individual can creatively and positively express selfhood. Institutional racism stifles black mental development, because

---

5   W. E. DuBois, *The Souls of Black Folk* (Fawcett Publishers, 1961), p. 17.

racism places blacks in the position of always reacting to whites rather than creating.

More importantly, because of racial oppression, life in the black community has become idle cyclical imitation, movement without positive direction, or independent thought. Collective imitation is indeed collective suicide.

On the one hand, programming the human mind is a relatively simple task. On the other, deprogramming the human mind is on the order of the miraculous. Indeed, blacks have become too complacent in their childlike ignorance. Living by another group's external value system, especially when that group's sole motivation is your destruction, invariably creates self-estrangement. Self-estrangement engenders hopelessness, and hopelessness creates a loss of integrity and moral character and a feeling of despair. Only to the degree that a group creates its own internal value system can it come to understand the limitlessness of the human spirit and the resourcefulness of the human mind. God did not create individuals as defenseless beings trapped in a world of treachery without a means of liberation. Living on a day-to-day basis creates a lack of positive direction.

Therefore, what exists in the black community are dead spirits in living organisms—i.e., the unhealthy social condition called *aimlessness*. Bread and butter are no longer the primary issues in the black community, but quality of life. The astounding rates of black-on-black crime, drug addiction, juvenile delinquency, divorce and separation, and homosexuality are a social testament to the kind of meaninglessness that exists in the black community. Indeed, once an individual eats of the "living bread," hunger ceases; when he drinks of the "living water," thirst for vanity ceases. The consciousness of "is-ness" is the antithesis to aimlessness and meaninglessness.

The Supreme Court decision to desegregate schools in 1954 has had a tremendously negative impact on the degree and kind of aimlessness in the black community. That is, the childhood innocence of blacks beguiled them into trusting the *words* of whites rather than creatively analyzing their *actions*. Integration as a legal tactic has been a skillfully contrived process of reindoctrination into the slave system, with the oppressors dictating the terms of human liberation. In short, integration was designed as a one-way street, because whites did not accept the humanity and divinity of blackness. Because whites had everything of positive cultural value and blacks had nothing of positive cultural value, blacks had to become like whites.

The institutional structure of an ethnic or racial group determines quality of life, because institutional structures determine job opportunities, life chances, and lifestyles. Historically then blacks are the only racial/ethnic group in American society that has had "special" institutional structures built for them, namely churches and schools. One might ask, why didn't whites feel that this gesture posed serious threats to the slave system? But the more important question is, why haven't blacks been able to creatively expand upon these institutional structures and use them as moral affirmations of their own personhood/peoplehood, liberation, and human dignity? Why haven't blacks developed an institutional counterculture, a focused "ought"? Instead blacks have been using these institutional structures as hiding places, seeking to avoid the harshness of racial oppression rather than creatively confronting it.

Religion should not confuse individuals about the meaning of life but rather clarify it. By no means should educational processes produce derelicts. Indeed, learning is about spiritual enlightenment. For example, approximately 80 percent of all the blacks in this country are educated in environments that are 80 to 100 percent black. At the same time, almost 65 percent of all PhDs granted to blacks are in the field of education, yet blacks are just as victimized by educational processes as any other minority group. Again, one might ask, what are blacks educating themselves for? Is the answer *extinction*?

Unfortunately, an increase in higher education degrees in the black community has not concomitantly yielded an increase in the ability of blacks to co-opt the social structure for their own collective survival. Blacks indeed have been too obsessed with the acquisition of external academic credentials and for too long have neglected the diligent pursuit of the internal CS degree—i.e., common sense. In short, blacks have neglected the kind of enlightenment that only comes when one sees with the eyes of the mind rather than the physical eyes. In American society, titles and power are not necessarily synonymous. It is unfortunate that so-called black intellectuals have not consistently disassembled and interpreted the meaning of the social structure for the black masses.

The phenomenal rise of mental illness in the black community is indicative of the lack of meaning and positive direction in the black community. Mental illness is a denial of consciousness ("is-ness"). There is no hiding place in American society from the ugliness of racial oppression. Those who break down simply choose to hide in themselves. Society can't get in and the individual chooses not to come out; he locks the door from the inside. Blacks are beginning to take on both the psychoses and neuroses of whites, which lead to total self-destruction.

It is time for a silent revolution, the process of transforming self and society without firing a shot. In other words, the time has come for a renaissance of the human spirit. We must call off the external fight for artificially contrived scarcities and take the fight to the internal battlefield; every individual must wrestle with his own human spirit. Every individual to some degree is a living paradox, both friend and foe, because he is the problem and, at the same time, the solution. This silent revolution will require a basic change in value orientations and a restructuring of institutional arrangements. The problem of social change is indeed perplexing because it involves changing human personalities.

The silent revolution has three important components: (1) knowledge, or locating the root cause of the problem, (2) understanding, or the creative power of independent thinking and analysis, and (3) self-love, or the ability to positively see self in others. The silent revolution has as its objectives two concrete goals: (1) the creation of an internal spiritual value system and moral order, and (2) the development of an egalitarian model of leadership, rather than an authoritarian model.

Finally, some elitist whites (not all whites) have declared an unrighteous materialistic war on ethnic minorities. We therefore must declare a righteous spiritual war on the institutional structures and value orientations of American society. That is, we must become intellectual warriors, because a slave should never die a natural death. A slave should never cease struggling to free his spirit and creative consciousness regarding the meaning of life. Indeed, individuals are born as God's truth and should never die as another person's lie. Again, to change is to die. In order to change, one must deny the self of today in order to pursue an unknown self of tomorrow. Strange and great are those who consciously kill themselves in order that they might live in the glory of God.

8 A PHILOSOPHICAL ANALYSIS OF BLACK ACADEMIA

Historically black colleges and universities (HBCUs) are dying, not because of external constraints, but rather because of internal chaos: governance and presidential leadership. In short, black colleges and universities are suffering from a serious lack of intellectual integrity and moral leadership. Indeed, black colleges continually expose black America to "dead knowledge"—i.e., knowledge irrelevant to the collective survival of urban twenty-first century America. Without a doubt, HBCUs are not actively involved in the communities in which they exist or in the resolution of real-world social problems. Black colleges have not been able to resolve the "town versus gown" dilemma.

Structurally, black colleges exist to serve black communities. When black colleges/universities do not creatively and adequately address social ills, they can be said to have their own problems of structure.

Problems of university governance are not caused by evil and/or corrupt university officials; rather, evil and/or corrupt university officials are allowed to flourish only in a bureaucratic system that tolerates and indeed rewards abuses of power. In short, most black colleges are not rationalized bureaucracies but personality-driven adhocracies. Such systems contribute to two problems of structure:

1. The difficulty of effective community-wide planning by black colleges
2. The problem of reordering community priorities in order to address such social ills as institutional racism, poverty, economic freedom, sexism, and inequality regarding political power.

The above structural problems are reflections of the pattern and distribution of power resources in the black community. To be sure, black colleges are elitist toward the external community, ultra-conservative toward internal changes, and above all conformist toward white institutional structures. To unravel these patterns and their dysfunctional social consequences, one must analyze the nature of higher education in American society.

THE PROBLEMS OF HIGHER EDUCATION: SOCIAL DEMOCRACY VERSUS ELITISM

Education in American society has an inherent dilemma. It has become the power tool for enhancing elitism, rather than social democracy, in American society. Therefore, the functions of American educational institutions have not changed concomitantly to address pressing new societal demands. Indeed, American educational institutions have boxed themselves into a static, materialistic, and elitist value orientation. In so doing, the educational enterprise does not facilitate creative learning and analytical thinking. In fact, an individual's education usually gets in the way of learning. The very nature of learning (openness) requires social democracy, and educational institutions are not social democracies but rather authoritarian systems.

Therefore, American educational institutions in general have not been able to implement a "community beyond the community" value orientation. The goal then of white colleges and universities has always been socio-political-economic elitism. Black colleges and universities, in their structural imitation of white educational institutions, have ended up with the same outcome—black elitism. While whites have their "ivory towers," blacks have their "ebony towers." Ironically, in a racist society there can never be such an entity as black elitism. So the question is, elitism in relationship to what? In the eyes of some whites, a black person, regardless of whether he or she has a PhD or no D, is still a "nigger." Education indeed does not reflect the idealized goals of social democracy, and this in and of itself presents a serious problem for American society.

9 THE DIFFICULTY OF EFFECTIVE COMMUNITY-WIDE PLANNING

Black colleges, just like their white counterparts, have boxed themselves into an institutional ethos of individualism. In so doing, they have turned inward to serve their own institutional ego interests. Individualism (self-centeredness) relativizes social reality. Racism is not an individual social phenomenon. Regardless of what individual whites seek to do to individual blacks, racism is a collective phenomenon. As a result, most blacks view black colleges as a place to learn how to "cross over"—i.e., to learn how to be accepted by whites rather than learn how to maximize individual potential.

Thus, the educational institutional model currently in use in black colleges conflicts with the needs of the larger black community. In other words, the model of higher education currently in use in the black college community was designed to perpetuate white supremacy (white elitism). The model colonizes knowledge. Knowledge is a source of power and control, and control of the flow of information is a key factor in maintaining a mental slave system. To be sure, the present model seriously interferes with the development of a pure ideological frame of reference, which in turn legitimizes the moral existence of black people.

In short, this organizational model effectively separates black colleges from black communities and creates fragmentation. As such, it also directly jeopardizes black freedom. After all, black freedom is not housed in white institutional structures and social processes but in self-help initiatives. To invariably imitate the "slave-master's" ways of doing things in a racist society is to mentally enslave the self.

THE PROBLEM OF REORDERING COMMUNITY PRIORITIES TO ADDRESS SOCIAL ILLS

American society has become highly credentialed and professionalized. In order to get a "good" job, formal educational credentials are a necessity. Increases in the size of black colleges and universities have led to even more bureaucratization, increased specialization, compartmentalization, and above all the neutralization of the effectiveness of college life. What is essentially non-material in nature (knowledge) has taken on the character of big business. Now even the academic enterprise is driven by economic forces rather than the acquisition of knowledge and skills. The value orientation of big business concerns itself with who gains and who loses in the exchange processes. Who gains and who loses in the exchange processes at black colleges? Black colleges, black students, the larger black community—or everyone?

The value orientation of education in the black community encourages individualism and materialism as a way of life. The self-centered value orientation of blacks is one of the root causes of social disorganization in the black community. As a result, higher education in the black community has taken on an ostrich-like attitude of avoidance—that is, the head is in the sand, but the hind parts are exposed. To be sure, black colleges have provided avenues of personal social mobility for the so-called talented few, but the many are still trapped in the ghettos of their own minds.

Black colleges rarely use their academic resources to help plan their own institutional futures--let alone the future of the larger black community. Black colleges have not been able to reorder community priorities because they have not developed an internal value orientation that on one hand legitimizes their own existence and on the other fosters interdependence rather than self-centeredness. Instead, black colleges have been helping to socialize the black community into a dependency status, thus remaining the foster children of white society.

Again, values dictate institutional forms and social processes, and self-centeredness appears to be the most salient value in the black community. (This value orientation is nourished not only by black colleges but also by black churches.) A social testament to the self-centered character of black colleges is the dysfunctional character of college alumni associations. It is a well-known fact that black college alumni associations, for the most part, are not actively involved in the lives of black colleges. Why? In part, the answer lies in the inability of black colleges to generate and maintain an interdependent value orientation. For four years, black colleges serve as surrogate family socializing agents. Therefore, black colleges ought to generate an enormous ethical investment capital in their graduates. Why then can't they enlist commitments from black students, which would invariably enhance their "reason for being"?

Given the collective social needs of the black community, black colleges have failed miserably in their efforts to address those needs. Black colleges were born out of social protest; therefore, the goal of black colleges should be social protest, not social conformity. It is apparent that black colleges have not embraced societal reform as a goal.

ADMINISTRATION VERSUS MANAGEMENT

The value orientation of black colleges has produced a distinctively managerial style and philosophy. Again, for the most part, black colleges are personality-driven organizational structures. Except in rare instances, black college officials are managers rather than administrators. Administration is concerned with structural functions and performance levels, and in order to function, its practitioners must have an open mind. Administration then is not merely policy decision making regarding resource allocation, but it is also the conscious sharing of power. Therefore, administration is about the conscious sharing of power and social cost accountability, while management is about the conscious hoarding of power, or turf building.

Administration involves high ideals and futuristic visions. When a bureaucratic structure stifles a focus on the future, it renders itself irrelevant. Management involves "holding the line" and dealing with mundane, everyday affairs. Indeed, both functions are necessary to attain goals effectively. Conversely, reward systems in black colleges are consciously skewed to favor power positions and titles rather than the learning process. In short, unity is virtually nonexistent in a managerial bureaucratic system. This is a serious dilemma, given that a college's most important goals ought to be (1) the initiation of students into the life of the mind, (2) the socialization of students into a commitment to use independent critical thinking skills and analysis to resolve problems, and (3) the development of students' technical competence and intellectual integrity.

The individualistic value orientation of black colleges engenders political power struggles centered upon getting and maintaining administrative positions, because rewards are skewed toward those positions. As a result, academic excellence for administrators becomes a "dirty word," and therefore it is all but nonexistent for faculty, staff, and students. After all, who are black college officials accountable to? By and large, black college officials abandon their primary task—intellectual scholarship—in order to avoid losing their administrative position(s). Without a doubt, black colleges are hostile bureaucratic structures, but in part they are maintained as such by black college officials. Either way, the result is that scholarship and intellectual creativity are lost in black colleges because black college officials fail to set examples of scholarship and intellectual integrity. Example is the only true teacher.

Couple this social fact with the slave heritage of blacks, and one can readily understand why blacks invariably institutionalize a love/hate syndrome in their bureaucratic structures. Because the ambivalence of simultaneous self-love and self-hate is not resolved on the individual level, due to the socialization processes in the black community, whenever blacks come together institutionally, social conflict rather than social cooperation predominates. When a marginal group operates out of a dominant group's value system, social conflict is inevitable because the marginal group does not have social control over what it values as a group. Because there is no basis for black authority in a racist society, it is difficult for blacks to positively embrace black leadership. Blacks are not conditioned to be compassionate to themselves and each other because, for the most part, blacks believe that they have no purpose for living in America other than to serve whites.

Black colleges then are characterized by the problem of management by emotional adhocracy, rather than administration by function. That is, management is not guided by futuristic, visionary, socio-spiritual objectives. It seems obvious that paramount attention must be given to human relations within black colleges and universities, as they themselves represent the interaction between human and non-human resources.

THE STANDARDIZATION OF CURRICULA

Learning begins at birth and should continue throughout the life cycle. College is not the "alpha and omega" of learning. In fact, increasingly college has become the epitome of *mis*education mainly because of its static curricula.

The standardization of curricula is apparent at most black colleges. The result is spoonfed education. Students are expected to absorb facts and ways of doing things and parrot them back to their professors. Helping students learn how to think independently and analyze critically is virtually nonexistent. Seemingly, the goal of black colleges is to eliminate creative tension and to induce idle imitation, the routinizing of thinking and acting. Dr. G. M. Sawyer, former president of Texas Southern University, states the problem eloquently:

> The recurring fault among us educators is that frequently we're overly committed to passing on a corpus of ideas in our instructional programs without adequately screening out those ideas that should be separated from the corpus—those that offer little use in a highly sophisticated, urban, futuristic society . . . .
>
> Here at TSU, I have some of the most personable associates among the faculty; they are absolutely charming. But some are presenting the same issues, saying the same old things, even using the same jokes to illustrate points long without relevance or importance. There are procedures and practices that would be perpetuated by some of this faculty that were obsolete even in the nineteenth century. A few seem so bent on keeping us in their dinosaur world that they fantasize rather than teach, and I imagine they perceive a student as a baby brontosaurus to be nurtured on a dinosaurian diet of obsolescence . . . .
>
> This isn't just true of some of our faculty; such regressive traits are to be found wherever educators assemble—from the halls of the most prestigious universities to the parking lots of the newest two-year college. And not only among educators, but among human beings generally. Most of man's institutions

are monuments to mediocrity, minutiae, and moments long past. It's just so obvious when this is true of us whose job is to guide the education of the young . . . .

Passing on a corpus of ideas is our reason for being, but woe on us who would pass on ideas and traits with a blind eye for imitation, oblivious to the demands of eras that have no precedence in world history . . . . Our commitment to urban development requires a courageous break from those traditions that would constrain us, and a bold imaginative leap into first, the present, then the most promising future that has ever been possible for mankind.[6]

Obviously, one of the most pressing concerns facing black colleges is the development of an instructional systems paradigm that will, among other things, provide a basis for relating degree, curricula, and course objectives to community needs. The instructional systems paradigm ought to describe and provide an intellectual framework for and structural-functional relationships between departmental objectives, college objectives, and above all real-world hierarchies. This paradigm should serve as a guide for purposes of experimentation, individuation, interdisciplinary studies, technology of instruction, inter-departmental studies, curricula design, and developmental processes within respective academic departments.

CONCLUSION

This essay has argued that black colleges have historically functioned in such a manner as to maintain the plantation system between blacks and whites. Within this context then black colleges have failed their own constituencies as well as the larger black community. Black colleges

---

6   Granville M. Sawyer, "One University's Urban Commitment," *The Journal of Extension,* Spring 1973, pp. 44–45.

have directly contributed to the void of moral leadership, the sense of intellectual meaninglessness (graveyard mentality), and the lack of positive direction rampant in the black community. After all, black colleges are supposed to serve as training grounds for the development of black leadership.

Increasingly, black colleges have become "freakhouses" and leisure-time resorts rather than the intellectual brain trust of the black community. "Freakiness" is culturally expressed in a wide array of lifestyles (e.g., dress, drug usage, college bands, and above all sexual expression). The driving question in some black college circles is, who can out-freak whom? Black colleges therefore represent an escape from social responsibility based in an understanding of human interdependence. Let me quickly add that if black colleges represent the *crème de la crème* of the black community, then it shouldn't surprise anyone that whites do not take blacks seriously. Black colleges must take a long hard look at the products they are producing and stop marketing degrees and begin to market careers.

Instead of leading social change, black colleges sanction existing social structures and routine ways of doing things and fail to create innovations. Therefore, a heavy inertia lies upon black colleges. If black colleges are to survive, they must affirm their interdependence with the larger black community, rethink their mission, alter their value orientations, and above all restructure their academic programs to effectively deal with the urban-suburban complex of social ills and the information explosion.

Black colleges cannot remain degree mills. Education must become a process of socio-spiritual enlightenment rather than merely the pursuit of a college degree. When this happens, black colleges will become living organisms that make a positive difference in the quality of life in the black community. A tireless and relentless quest for truth is the only meaningful basis for human community. Truth creates life simply because truth is eternal. Black colleges cannot continually feed themselves on a diet of lie-accommodations.

Finally, I might add, the exception is not the rule, nor is the exception the problem, but rather the problem is caused by the rule. In other words, there are some black colleges that are doing an outstanding job, and of course they represent the exception rather than the rule.

10 HOW TO WRECK A UNIVERSITY

There's nothing like authoritative ignorance.
—Brickman

1. Employ personnel who are not capable emotionally or intellectually of implementing the conceptual framework (philosophy) of the university.
2. Compete internally for resources, both human and nonhuman, as though the university's existence is not grounded in the same mandate, philosophy, and goals.
3. Be oblivious to the social fact that planning and evaluation are systematic processes.
4. Be oblivious to the social fact that evaluation data impact social change.

5. Violate established systems, processes, and procedures that are designed to rationalize and make efficient the operations of the university.

6. Do not establish an inquiry design in order to encourage input by various units and individuals into university decision-making processes (such as policy decisions).

7. Alienate individuals from power resources within the university structure.

8. Encourage the concepts of "us" and "them" in intra/interpersonal relationships, power and authority relationships, and staff and line positions.

9. Encourage artificial and arbitrary distinctions that enhance racism, sexism, and general/specific incompetence.

10. Encourage behaviors that violate human rights, civil rights, and human integrity—that is, encourage behaviors that are not related philosophically to and are inconsistent with what the university is supposedly about.

11. Establish goals on a "post hoc ergo propter hoc" or after-the-fact basis, which encourages inefficiency and lack of accountability.

12. Deal in "strange variables," where a variable is a property characteristic of a unit of analysis that takes on different values across different units of analyses. (Strange, wouldn't you say?)

One question comes to mind: Is there a discrepancy between what is and what ought to be at Texas Southern University? If so, do we have the critical thinking ability, institutional strategies, and the will to bridge the gap? This question is not raised as a medium to run down TSU philosophically, institutionally, and programmatically. On the contrary, it is raised in order to provide a conceptual framework for some creative thinking and/or ideas about the following issues:

- Institutional planning and coordination (programmatic and collegiate)
- University evaluation (institutional, collegiate, and professional)
- Systems analysis and systems integration
- Institutional strategies for positive changes
- Crosscultural and multiethnic education (equality versus elitism in higher education)
- Inter/intra group communication
- Inter/intra staff communication (equality versus elitism)
- Community-based educational programs (outpost centers)
- Curriculum development and community needs assessment
- Human values and urbanism as a way of life

Not being clear about these issues as a university puts us at the same starting point as an ill-advised sprinter who runs about in circles creating motion and chaos, but never a university community.

Prometheus

An end to words. Deeds now.
The world is shaken.
The deep and secret way of thunder is rent apart. Fiery wreaths of
*   lightning flash.*
Whirlwinds toss the swirling dust.
The blasts of all the winds are battling in the air, and sky and sea
*   are one.*
On me the tempest falls.
It does not make me tremble.
O holy Mother Earth, O air and sun, behold me. I am wronged.
**   —Aeschylus**

We can revitalize Texas Southern University if we receive the spirit that is embodied in that old Negro spiritual: "It's me. It's me. It's me, O Lord! Standing in the need of prayer!" In other words, the spirit of self-renewal.

It's not the BOARD OF REGENTS—it's me, Lord!

It's not the OFFICE OF THE PRESIDENT—it's me, Lord!

It's not the OFFICE OF THE PROVOST—it's me, Lord!

It's not the DEANS—it's me, Lord!

It's not the PROFESSORS—it's me, Lord!

It's not the CIVIL SERVICE STAFF—it's me, Lord! It's not the STUDENTS—it's me, Lord! It's not the BLACK FOLKS—it's me, Lord! It's not the WHITE FOLKS—it's me, Lord! It's not the RICH FOLKS—it's me, Lord! It's not the POOR FOLKS—it's me, Lord! It's not the DEMOCRATS—it's me, Lord! It's not the REPUBLICANS—it's me, Lord!

It's not the UNIVERSITY OF TEXAS—it's me, Lord! Standing in the need of prayer: self-renewal.

What lives have we if we have not life together? For there is no life that is not lived in human community, and no human community that is not lived under God's reality, where equal is equal, not more or less equal (the social meaning of death).

AUTHOR'S NOTE

I have an undergraduate degree from an HBCU: Barber-Scotia College in Concord, North Carolina. All of my graduate degrees are from majority-white institutions: Colgate-Rochester Crozer Divinity School (BD), the University of Rochester (MA), and Syracuse University (PhD). My initial college/university teaching experiences were in majority-white institutions in the states of New York and Illinois.

After meditating on making a real difference in the lives of young blacks, I decided to complete my teaching career in an HBCU. I chose Texas

Southern University in Houston, Texas, based upon the recommendations of personal friends. I wrote the above essay, "How to Wreck a University," after being at TSU for two weeks. After one year, I wrote the essay "A Philosophical Analysis of Black Academia." Not long afterward, the president of the university notified me by certified mail that I was terminated. Later I informed him that I was going to get him fired, since he did not hire himself as the president. I hadn't known that TSU was his personal plantation, but I was not his personal slave.

My understanding of reality was that TSU was a taxpayer and state-supported public institution of higher learning based upon the cornerstone principle of "academic freedom." Subsequently, I garnered student support, and we initiated a spiritual "Jericho March" around the university daily with the Bible as our weapon of choice. Six months later the president was fired. The truth of God can work miracles even in the dysfunctional politics of public higher education.

Later I was rehired at the university and immediately labeled by administrative officials as an outside radical. I should add, however, that the president did apologize for his ungodly behavior after he was terminated. After all, justice is a spiritual concept, not revenge; it is written that individuals reap what they sow. And, of course, I accepted his apology, because forgiveness is divine.

11 BLACK INTELLECTUALS: MYTH OR REALITY?

The purpose of this essay is not to condemn black intellectuals but to present an idea whose time is long overdue: collective responsibility. It is indeed extended family reunion time.

It is hoped that the ideas presented in this essay will provide an intellectual framework for some creative thinking about the following issues: (1) how best to educate, and (2) the development of a countercultural philosophy and intellectual strategies that facilitate interdependence rather than negative, individualistic materialism (that is, the "each to his own way" philosophy).

Black people are universally confronted with one overriding social need: to stop their ethnic/cultural dehumanization. Any attempt to generate intellectual strategies to stop the cultural dehumanization of blacks by whites, and blacks by blacks, must begin with an empirical analysis of the extent to which blacks are involved in their own cultural dehumanization. That is, if one is marginal in a dominant culture, there are two choices that can be exercised: (1) culturally imitate and (2) culturally generate. The following model serves as a guide to illuminate the issue and ideally engender further models.

Without a doubt, white culture and its concomitant institutional structure are repressive, depressive, and oppressive in nature. That is, American culture is an unacceptable, arbitrary reality for blacks. Indeed, American institutional arrangements are somewhat dysfunctional even for many whites. It is extremely important for blacks to find creative ways to "reconstruct" reality. How do you transform collective interests into collective action?

Relatively speaking, there are two institutions in the black community: black churches and black colleges and universities. Black churches have been the cornerstone of black culture. Unfortunately, in the twenty-first century, too many black churches have long since been co-opted by the greed, envy, materialism, personal jealousy, and negative individualism of many black religious leaders. At this time, blacks are wandering in the wilderness of non-productivity spiritually, morally, and economically without a deliverer. Couple this social fact with the extremely low level of formal schooling among some black religious leaders, and the black church becomes a veritable obstacle to interdependence in the black community.

For this reason, the logical place to begin the countercultural process is in the black college subsystem. By "countercultural process" I mean the process of establishing new sets of values, new institutional forms, new structures, new ideologies, new ways of thinking and organizing knowledge, and above all a new worldview. In short, it is the process of demythologizing white-dominant culture through an existential assessment of its cultural strengths and weaknesses. The notion of a counterculture implies selective integration and assimilation rather than blind acceptance. Cultural imitation engenders self-estrangement and self-alienation.

Counterculture implies antithesis rather than thesis. The thesis is the "cultural dehumanization" of blacks by whites. Black oppression is a cultural constant rather than a cultural relative. To become cultural imitators of whites is invariably to participate in one's own harassment. Without an antithesis (counterculture) to the thesis (cultural dehumanization), there can never be a viable synthesis. It is for this reason that integration has not worked for blacks, but rather against their collective survival. Because blacks have not developed countervailing power resources, we have not been able to meaningfully affect the nature of our collective experience with whites. Blacks have not been able to develop their communities and institutions because blacks have not had managerial control over power resources.

Unfortunately, blacks were programmed to self-hate because of chattel slavery and the loss of knowledge of self. The human mind is indeed delicate. If any group lacks control over its God-given power resource (personal thought processes), then priorities become confused. The ability to live a meaningful life depends upon the ability to set priorities and deal with self-discipline, because the lack of self-discipline is the devil. When control over personal thought processes is lost, the only social role one can play is that of prostitution. Too many blacks have confused outward appearance with inward reality. What is on the inside of individuals creates what is on the outside. Culture is a reflection of internal values.

In the past, the dominant ideological theme for most blacks has been integration into mainstream culture as a means of stopping their dehumanization. Unfortunately, there was not an intelligent assessment of the social costs of integration. Indeed, the price tag has been much too high. Integration is a methodology, not an ideology. Throughout the

1960s, this confusion of methodology with ideology resulted in mass confusion in the black community.

Genuine integration implies the parties involved have mutually agreed that each has cultural strengths and cultural weaknesses. Cultural positives (strengths) will be integrated, and cultural negatives (weaknesses) will be overlooked. Moreover, genuine integration can only take place with perceived equals. Because blacks did not have a countercultural movement that provided an antithesis to the prevailing thesis, whites defined the terms of integration. They controlled the tactics, strategies, and indeed the entire rule book—the law. Therefore, in the so-called integration process, whites did not have to give up anything, particularly their "old white ways"; they only had to sophisticatedly disguise them.

Within this process, blacks were effectively saying, "We have no cultural positives (strengths), so we will become like whites." Naturally, this was alright with whites because it made their job easier. So since 1954 whites have been granting blacks the privilege of becoming white without the privileges associated with being white—that is, if you can become white. Thus, if a marginal group makes sacred a dominant group's culture, then the marginal group glorifies the dominant group and its culture as godlike in character. That is, the marginal group participates in its own self-annihilation. When whites created the "social bed" of integration, they assumed a diagonal position in the bed. Obviously, if one gets in the bed diagonally, he does not intend for another to sleep with him comfortably.

Black bodies have been off the plantation for quite some time, but black minds to some degree are still in chains. Could it be that blacks became so overjoyed with the social fact that whites freed the slaves that they forgot who enslaved the slaves? Freedom is not free—i.e., void of individual and collective responsibility and social-cost accountability. Freedom is a God-given right, not a civil right. Blacks for too long have been beguiled into looking to whites for their socio-economic salvation and freedom. Salvation comes from within, not without. Whites simply moved the slave system from the plantation fields to factory warehouses, from the countryside to city sidewalks, and from the family system to the college and church systems.

Since 1954, whites have been using the integration tactic as "sucker-psychology" games designed solely to maintain the civil-servant relationship between whites and blacks. The dominant culture through the propagandist research of the Moynihans, Jencks, and Jensens of the world has consistently played on the cultural weaknesses and stereotypes associated with being black through their "blaming the victim" theories. If the goal of blacks has been to achieve symbolic whiteness, what else should whites talk about other than the "shortcomings" of blacks?

Indeed, it is a difficult process to convert from physical blackness to physical whiteness. Actions speak louder than words. Even though whites are mainly responsible for many of the cultural weaknesses of blacks, they take no responsibility for the cultural demise of blacks. Rather than continuing to use force to colonize black labor, whites colonized black labor by colonizing black minds. That is, whites have been using black churches and black educational institutions to colonize black minds, in order to control black bodies (i.e., exploit black labor).

Traditionally, the black church has been concerned with life in the "by and by," while the white church concerns itself with life in the "here and now." This is precisely why eleven o'clock on Sunday morning is still the most segregated hour in American society. Black educational institutions are self-instructional courses in how best to imitate whites. Black college life is an imitation of white culture. That is, the experiential ethos of black college life is self-centeredness, competition, independence, separateness, and authoritarian control. Black colleges and universities indeed do not foster collective social responsibility, interdependence, commonality, and collective survival. Unfortunately, black colleges and universities perpetuate the cultural ethos of survival of the fittest rather than collective interdependence. Thus black institutions are designed to delude blacks into thinking that they can avoid the unavoidable, which is death (physically or materially).

It is within this context that I shall discuss the black intellectual's betrayal of his own humanity. Obviously, I am not suggesting that all black intellectuals have always unquestioningly accepted dominant white culture. Antithetical thought can be found in the works of such black intellectuals as W. E. B. DuBois, E. Franklin Frazier, Henry A. Bullock, Harold Cruse, and so on. Although these individuals are representative of black critical thought, this list is by no means exhaustive.

The question at hand is, what role have intellectual traditions played in accurately presenting real-world hierarchies for black intellectuals, black students, and above all the black community? Indeed, given present socio-political economic arrangements, mainstream intellectual thought has done at worst a disservice and at best a miserable job of providing blacks with useful kinds of knowledge. In his book *Towards the Sociology of Knowledge*, Gunter Remmling presents a dazzling historical account of intellectual life, which culminates in an account of present-day thought patterns and worldviews.

> Throughout history, intellectuals have done more to obscure the relationship between human existence and thought than to reveal it. By accepting dominant political and socio-economic arrangements they have deflected the analytical thrust of their cerebral power from the bedrock of existential reality; by correlating their activities and their productions with trans-temporal spirit and values, ideas, and ideals, intellectuals have sanctified their failures as diagnosticians of social-historical life situations. The defensive preoccupation of mainstream intellectuals with emanations from a fabricated higher reality gave birth to a conveniently bewildering plethora of concepts

which include incantations such as structure, equilibrium, order, consensus, tradition, authority, objectivity, validity, reliability. . . . These concepts rendered ridiculous by actual political, social, and economic behavior . . . have been dressed up in the musty robes of theology, the threadbare raiment of philosophy, and the mod costumes of mathematics.[7]

G. W. Remmling is referring to the defensive and reactionary stance of white intellectuals. White intellectuals indeed describe "what is" and rarely ever suggest "what ought to be." There are lies, damn lies, and some white intellectuals who are pros at how to "lie with statistics." Instead of challenging these white intellectuals, some black intellectuals imitate them.

Black colleges and universities, the editorial policies of black journals, and the structure of thought in the black community all are reflections of the materialism of white culture. In so doing, black intellectuals pathologically reinforce materialism over humanity, individualism over interdependence, value neutrality over commitment, ignorance over spiritual enlightenment, and above all ideological authoritarianism over political radicalism. It is clear then that most black intellectuals participate in the intellectual genocide of black people, and more importantly, the cultural demise of black Americans. Black intellectuals have not been, for the most part, asking the right questions.

The existential reality of the "black experience" ought to be a causal stimulus for "black mental configurations," not white mental configurations. Black intellectuals have been too obsessed with physical and material death, and as a result they are dead intellectually. Death is a social fact—one in which an individual has no choice. Life then is not about avoiding death. Life is about creative and meaningful living. For one's death only illuminates the meaning of his or her life.

---

7   G. W. Remmling, *Towards the Sociology of Knowledge* (New York: Humanities Press, 1973).

It is ironic that black people are so easily persuaded by lies (unreality) rather than the truth (reality). Individualism relativizes the truth. In an individualistic culture, truth is always conditioned by "partial perspectives," or the tunnel vision of beholders. Knowledge is a quest for truth. Life is about learning. Learning is about the open competition of ideas and the integration of ideas. When lies are institutionalized as truths, it is the role of creative thinkers to begin to set the record straight. Black intellectuals must free themselves from the social need to be legitimized by white intellectuals, white journals, white professional organizations, and so on, in order to come from among the ranks of the "walking-dead club." Institutional arrangements define what constitutes "professionalism," and until black intellectuals can influence the structure and function of institutional arrangements, the only profession a black has is that of being professionally black. And if one is black in a racist society, then he or she has not met the first qualification of belonging to that society—i.e., being white.

Black intellectuals must begin to orchestrate a countercultural intellectual movement. That is, black intellectuals must begin to reconstruct reality for an oppressed class of people, not perpetuate unreality. The black college, just like the black church, is a stop-gap institution, a means of keeping blacks from becoming radically politicized. In recent decades, there were two notable black intellectual giants: Martin Luther King Jr. and Malcolm X. Ironically, the black college subsystem created one and the American penal system created the other.

The role of black intellectuals and black colleges of necessity must be more profound than that of white intellectuals and colleges. The role of black intellectuals and colleges is nation-building, i.e., developing its own cultural worldview. Black colleges in the past have provided avenues of individual mobility for blacks. The problem has never been the need for individual mobility, but group social mobility. Whites will always have need of "showcase tokens," because whites do not want to think that they are as inhumane as the social structure they created.

Thus neither the black church nor the black college has been able to generate a counterculture based on interdependence. Black colleges must imitate less and generate more. Black intellectuals must accept less and do more critical and analytical thinking. Black preachers must "whoop" less and instruct more. Above all, black churches must comfort less and challenge more. The basis for a black having a meaningful job in America cannot be that he or she is willing to be used as a tool to exclude other blacks. Until this perceived social fact is altered, blacks have no viable basis for their own collective existence.

Ideas about how best to educate have come from white intellectuals. Models such as the open school, open classroom, free school, continuous progress, magnet school, and so on have come from upper-class whites who want to pass on to their children a measure of "freedom" they never experienced. On the one hand, white alternate forms of education represent a rejection of traditional education values and structures. On the other hand, they represent more sophisticated ways to perpetuate the "same ole, same ole": the status quo. For there is nothing covered which will not be unveiled, and nothing hidden that will not be known.

Blacks have not been able to assess and model their cultural strengths because a lot of the negativism in the black ethos is indirectly or directly caused by blacks. Therefore, until blacks parse out the effects of internal negativism, there will never be an understanding of external negativism, nor how to minimize and counteract its effects. Escapism is not the solution to the horrible mess we are in; collective responsibility is.

Many blacks may seek to discredit the ideas presented in this essay by labeling them as negative or anti-black. Many whites may simply declare that I am an angry black man. I would like to point out one social fact. It is not the cultural positives and strengths in the black community that are the sources of our collective problems, but rather the cultural negatives. Therefore, until there is a clear understanding of the *internal* causes of social disorganization in the black community, there can be no real appreciation of cultural strengths. The cultural strengths of blacks tend to be obscured by both internal and external negativism. Negativism invariably generates negativism. Once again, not to be clear about the issues presented in this essay puts us at the same starting point as an ill-advised sprinter who runs about in circles, creating motion and chaos, and reaching the finish line only by accident, if ever. Freedom is always housed in self-initiative. We all know there is no such thing as Santa Claus.

BIBLIOGRAPHY

The Authorized King James Version of the Christian Bible. National Bible Press, Philadelphia.

Bullock, Henry A. *The History of Negro Education in the South.* Harvard University Press, 1967.

Cruse, Harold. *The Crisis of the Negro Intellectual.* New York: Morrow Press, 1967.

DuBois, W. E. B. *The Souls of Black Folk.* New York: Washington Square Press, 1930.

Frazier, E. Franklin. *The Negro in the United States.* New York: Macmillan Press, 1957.

Ladner, Joyce. *The Death of White Sociology.* New York: Random House, 1973.

Remmling, G. W. *Towards the Sociology of Knowledge.* New York: Humanities Press, 1973.

12 THE SOCIOLOGY OF "PARTY DOWN": SATURDAY NIGHT VERSUS SUNDAY MORNING

The ubiquity of nightclubs and churches in the black community is apparent even to the casual observer. This social fact alone raises some serious questions about the black mindset. Without a doubt, the modern black mindset is grounded in an escapism that is oriented toward the avoidance of pain and the maximizing of pleasure. Racial oppression has forced blacks into orienting their priorities (values), attitudes, and above all their lifestyles toward maximizing the pleasure principle. Yet to become a slave to pleasure is to deny that there are other dimensions of human existence. Life is multidimensional in nature. Indeed, the things that hurt, instruct.

Racism is a fundamental principle of American society, not an aberration. Its social consequences on human development have been devastating, to say the least. In an attempt to deny the reality of racism, blacks have become master builders of fantasy worlds. But to deny reality is tantamount to self-denial, a denial of being.

Partying in the black community is like unto the actions of the caterpillar in *Alice in Wonderland,* who seeks to give meaning to something that has no meaning. After all, partying is "organized" unorganized B.S. The most salient value in the black community seems to be "party down." The time is long overdue for somebody to say down with "party down" and up with some positive, collective, intellectual survival strategies. Blacks must stop deluding themselves, because whites are consciously aware not only of what is but, more importantly, of how what is came to be. The ostrich syndrome has taken blacks to the other side of midnight.

Values dictate institutional structures. Therefore, institutional structures in the black community are built upon this party-down mentality (value orientation). Black clubs, churches, and colleges all perpetuate this mentality. The party-down mentality is crystallized in the communal events of black fraternities and sororities. Black fraternities and sororities rarely, if ever, seek to directly influence communal action that is the political and economic structure of the black community. So-called middle-class blacks have been partying so hard that they have partied across the gender line and back before coming silently to rest in intra-sexuality, or the "freaky-deaky" process. Partying is indeed the epitome of living in unreality. It does not resolve institutional racism, political power inequality, economic inequality, sexism, or any other "ism." Again, these social problems are real in their social consequences, not imaginary.

Black nightclubs and black churches are flipsides of the same coin. Indeed, both serve as a mechanism to reduce psychological tension in order to militate against the evil that blacks see in whites, themselves, and the world. Black nightclubs serve as nighttime fantasies, and black churches serve as daytime fantasies. In the black church, the line between some black preachers and black comedians is so blurred that it is virtually impossible to differentiate one from the other. Both social roles are about entertainment, putting on a "show" to an unfriendly world. The questions are: Are there real differences between disco-dancing and shouting? Are there real differences between the genres of popular gospel and rhythm and blues? (The beat is the same; only the lyrics differ.) Without a doubt, the atmospheres in black churches and clubs are similar in nature, because both serve as a means of escape.

Just as values dictate institutional structures, institutional structures determine life chances, lifestyles, and developmental employment opportunities. Therefore, it is no coincidence that for many years Motown Records was the largest black-owned corporation in American society. Nor should it surprise anyone that historically the second-largest corporation in the black community was a picture-oriented magazine dealing with cosmetic manure. The fact that the economic and social structures of the black community are based upon entertainment rather than human development (individualistic economics rather than corporate economics) explains why blacks have an economy based upon stealing from one another, rather than an economic system based upon cooperation.

These individualistic economic structures also function in such a manner as to maintain both economic and residential segregation. In fact, clubs and churches extract resources from the black community but rarely if ever return any resources. But, more importantly, the entertainment mentality produced by these structures is directly related to the collective non-productivity of the black community: blacks party in time, on time, between time, and all the time. Institutional structures in the black community are based on and produce nonsense. Partying does not foster the courage to be black or an internalized sense of black awareness. To be sure, blacks are partying themselves into extinction.

The entertainment mentality and value orientation of blacks stifles intellectualism as well as economic growth (futurism). Blacks are caught up in the "follies of the times" and therefore are not constructing a living endowment for future generations of blacks. Rather than investing ethical, moral capital in black youth, we are partying away the future of our children.

In short, blacks are hustling backwards. Black clubs and black churches are none other than stopgap measures designed solely to insulate blacks from the harshness of racial oppression. While partying may serve as an accommodation process to help blacks adjust to their social condition, racial injustice, it does little to eliminate that social condition. Partying becomes a way to escape from institutional racism and its related consequences, rather than deal with them. Escapism cannot contribute to human development. To be sure, human development requires analytical thinking and productivity, not vain consumption. In fact, the preponderance of clubs and churches is an indicator of the "tunnel vision" of blacks, lack of creative intelligence, and institutional cooperation in the black community. The survival of a race of people cannot be centered on an entertainment-based value system. It is understandable that a child might be afraid of darkness, but it is incomprehensible that adults are afraid of the light, the Spirit of Truth.

Freedom and reality are synonymous. In fact, truth frees. Black freedom then is housed in self-initiatives. Partying as a value orientation maintains the economic slave system between blacks and whites and above all keeps blacks in a perpetual state of childhood innocence. We must develop ourselves or else we will institute the "last dance," a crude and bawdy version of collective suicide. If blacks are to survive, the party-down value orientation must be replaced with more realistic, spiritual, and moral values such as self-reliance, self-confidence, competence, intellectual integrity, and so on.

Of course, all work and no play makes Jack and Jill dull. But all play and no work makes Jack and Jill stupid and non-productive.

13

A SOCIO-RELIGIOUS ANALYSIS OF THE SOCIAL COSTS OF INSTITUTIONAL RACISM IN A THEORETICAL DEMOCRACY

We the willing, led for so long by the incompetent, have been doing nothing too long with so much; we must now attempt what was always possible: collective interdependence.

—Anonymous

T he fundamental problem for American society is institutional and corporate racism. Racism poses some perplexing questions. Why does it exist? What is its social cost? How can it be eliminated? The social pathology of racism invades society like cancer, spreading moral bankruptcy, economic waste, occupational mediocrity, and political stagnation.

What is racism? Racism in American society is a cultural religion. It has its mythology (white supremacy), its symbol (physical whiteness), its ideology (the exploitation and dehumanization of non-whites), and its institutions. The foundation of racism is human economic exploitation. It stems from "idealism and materialism," as manifested in Western socio-religious, philosophical axiology and the rise of the modern capitalist state. From the very beginning, humankind, in attempts to explain "what is," "what ought to be," and "how what is came to be," created religion as a meaning system, and some racial groups anthropologically depicted God in their own image (ethnocentrism) in order to exploit other human beings. The notion of the "stranger" gave rise to social myths and belief systems that set the historical stage for the black/white encounter.

Racism in America is about privilege without responsibility, restricting access to valued resources on the basis of racial and ethnic origin. At its root, racism (the economic exploitation of humans) is a negative idea, and it includes a series of negative correlates, namely (1) whites' negative view of themselves, and (2) blacks' negative view of themselves. Thus, racial oppression in America is a self-fulfilling prophecy.

Racism poses five overriding dilemmas:

1. Loss of national purpose
2. Economic waste
3. Occupational mediocrity
4. Political stagnation
5. Political confusion

Human economic exploitation and human community are incompatible concepts. Inconsistency breeds moral decay and moral bankruptcy, cynicism, a loss of spirituality, and above all a loss of national purpose (social meaning). Exclusion invariably costs more than inclusion.

Christianity provides very powerful ideas about community as well as personal and collective character development. However, whites betrayed Christianity and used it as an imperialistic tool in order to exploit non-whites. Because the value orientation of Western societies is based upon human economic exploitation, now whites are trapped by their own social history, their own symbols of success, and their institutional structures. The 1960s showed clearly what it means to be white, and many whites didn't like the image that was reflected on the "tube." Therefore, the 1960s depicted a need for personal and institutional liberation. Whites raised the question: are we like the "social structure" we have created? The answer was yes. So whites began a process to personally and institutionally liberate themselves through the Civil Rights Movement.

The process is incomplete. Whites are still in dire need of both personal and institutional liberation. Personal liberation must come first. Whites must culturally "de-whitize" themselves in order to free their minds and morally integrate mind and body. By "de-whitize" I mean that whites must give up their cultural sense of whiteness, not their biological whiteness, in order to become human. They must, in other words, learn to live beyond their physical whiteness. It's a difficult process because it requires a change of self-concept. Because of scientific and technological advances, whites must give up their "old white ways" and identify with the oppressed and disinherited in the universe.

Only then will whites discover the truth about themselves, others, the universe, and above all God. Personal liberation is an absolute because whites have become so negative about themselves, others, the universe, and God that they have the world on a downhill negative collision course that will lead straight to self-annihilation. Modern negative technology (e.g., the nuclear bomb) necessitates the nonviolent resolution of conflict. Institutional liberation will require a changing of symbols because institutional symbols are based on notions of white supremacy and non-white subjugation. Institutional liberation means a basic value reorientation, a reordering of national priorities, and a redistribution of the power resources in society. Whether whites can do it is the question of questions.

In fact, whites can initiate the process of institutional liberation only if they recover a sense of the spiritual, the power that is within the Christian tradition. The church was the one institution given to individuals for personal and collective character development (socialization). But whites used the church to exploit rather than to build human community. Whites must rediscover religion as a social phenomenon and come to understand its appropriateness for modern industrial societies.

Economic processes in American society motivate all social processes, and therefore an analysis of the economic structure of American society is crucial to an understanding of social ills. American economic policies are motivated by the exploitation of special units and individuals, which by definition creates deliberate waste, inefficiency, and incompetence.

Racism in its systematic institutional form became pervasive with the rise of mercantilism and capitalism. It eventually became crystallized in the Western world in order to justify the economic exploitation of people with "permanent tans."

However, this is not to say that the sole cause of racism is economic exploitation, and deny the existence of social, cultural, and political forces on either side of the racial continuum. Racism, just like sexism, is one of the many ways individuals seek to institute privilege in the human community in order to exploit. Economic processes in American society are viewed as an end in and of themselves, rather than a means to an end.

Economic policies motivated by the ideology of human exploitation create at least four problems:

(1) **A loss of workers' control, which is central to social democracy.** Increasing workers' control invariably means democratizing society. The notion of workers' control suggests both rationality and efficiency in the workplace and society. Obviously, it is an idea long since buried by American corporate business values and corporate greed. Profit is not evil, but institutionalized greed is. In this context, the ordinary citizen feels estranged and alienated from processes of government, dehumanized by work, and above all exploited by the economic system. (To be sure, politicians are the high priests of the greedy.)

(2) **A lack of market accountability to consumers.** National priorities are not established by the American voting populace but by the corporate system, which negates participatory democracy due to the use of political action committees (PACs). Thus the marketplace is based on the problematic value of corporate self-interest, which in turn necessitates the lack of accountability of the market to consumers. Industrial workers have minimal control over the quality and cost of products that are produced for consumption in the marketplace because of the influence of corporations on political processes and the profit motive. Thus, the American economic system creates privilege, inequity, pollution and waste, non-competition (monopolies), and above all the market's inability to respond to the needs of the underclass (i.e., minorities and poor individuals). Capitalism (rugged individualism) and interdependence (human community) are radical polar opposites.

(3) **Racism implies privilege and therefore stifles natural competition (self-competition).** Racism creates "occupational mediocrity" because it detracts individuals away from real work: self-realization, self-actualization, self-development, and nation-statehood. Work then becomes privilege rather than collective cooperative responsibility. And the question becomes, who's deciding the functional importance of occupations in relationship to the ongoing collectivity (society), and on the basis of what value system?

(4) **National planning, social coordination (systems integration), and people control become impossible.** In fact, all three are inherently impossible in a political system that values free enterprise (external competition), decentralization, and above all privilege for a few whites in a society that is multiethnic and multiracial. Racism engenders political stagnation because those who become political leaders want privilege without collective responsibility and social-cost accountability. The politics of race is alive and well in American society.

The human value of exploitation and "either/or" logic that undergird political processes are designed to perpetuate privilege, or individual survival versus collective survival. Racism ensures that government processes will always be in the hands of a minority of white males. In this respect, American society is no different from many authoritarian regimes. Hence, power in American society is structured according to the interests of a few elitist whites and therefore creates the unaccountability of power that weakens democratic institutions and society in general.

In fact, the structure of political parties is designed to militate against participatory and representative democracy. This process keeps "foreign ideas" out of the ranks of policy leadership and minimizes the debating of issues and the open competition of ideas. Politics in society is more about race and social class than self-consciousness (individual/social meaning).

As stated earlier, racism as a social system militates against the possibility that the most competent and qualified persons will get the most important jobs. Work is not meaningful because it is subjected to the whims of privilege: nepotism, favoritism, and above all the "buddy system." Most competent and efficient individuals do want administrative positions, as evident in the political gaming that takes place in bureaucratic structures (i.e., the Peter Principle). Because social processes are designed to exploit "work," modern individuals are obsessed with "leisure"—getting away from work as though work were ungodly and unholy.

Therefore, racism negates the functional theory of social stratification, an analysis of the division of labor in society, and concomitant social factors. The most competent and qualified individuals, more often than not, do not get the most important jobs in society. In fact, in American society the notion of social mobility is oftentimes conceptual justification for social inequality, a way to rationalize the vast inequity of opportunity in the social structure. Racial and ethnic groups are not seen as central and persistent elements in American society. Nor is racial and ethnic oppression viewed as an independent causal dynamic in society. Social stratification is not just an economic phenomenon but a social phenomenon as well, moral and cultural in nature.

Thus, in light of all of the above, the notion of privilege (institutional racism) militates against occupational efficiency, occupational competence, collectivism, and above all democracy as collective interdependence.

Vulgar capitalism (the institutionalization of the greed factor) and institutional racism as ideas are obsolete social systems. Social processes designed to exploit create violence, and our modern negative forms of technology necessitate the nonviolent resolution of conflict. If America and the world at large are to survive, we must take a giant *leap of faith* to integrate ideas in order to integrate cultures, socio-political systems, and above all *life*. Because the social cost of economic inequality is social chaos. But the concept of economic opportunity means universal happiness and social stability. Indeed, life is about happiness and an internalized peace of mind, both personally and societally.

14 WHITE SUPREMACY: MYTH OR REALITY?

L ike racism, the notion of white supremacy also stands as a fundamental obstacle to world peace and international moral order. As such, we must ask the same questions we asked of racism: How did it get started? What are its socio-cultural costs? How can the notion of white supremacy be eliminated?

Without a doubt, the basis for white existence has been institutionalized racial superiority. Yet the concept of race is a mental delusion because popular ideas about racial categories lack scientific biological objectivity. In other words, racial categories are conditioned by political systems rather than empirical biogenetic evidence. In fact, any cultural definition of race, racist or otherwise, lacks scientific validity.

Unlike ethnocentrism, racism is not a universal phenomenon. Most societies exhibit ethnocentrism in that members of all societies tend to think highly of themselves, but their self-concepts are based on cultural differences rather than biological or genetic differences. One can be ethnocentric without being racist. But unfortunately in many instances racism has become the basis for social definitions and political constructs. Social definitions dictate normative behavior and cultural socialization. When racial superiority forms the basis of social definitions, it invariably undermines the culture, particularly in terms of the development of spiritual values (i.e., moral, internal values).

The overwhelming weight of empirical evidence suggests that white supremacy is a social myth, one perpetuated by both whites and non-whites alike. Of course, if certain individuals are biologically superior to others, then the Judeo-Christian conception of God must invariably be called into question. Did God create inequality and is therefore responsible for it? Also, if whites are biologically superior, why did they institutionalize inequality? The natural thing would have been to have an open-ended social system and to allow open-ended competition for scarce resources (based on natural selection and survival of the fittest).

Much of what we know about biology we didn't know one hundred fifty years ago. Then, as well as now, social scientists in the field of race and biogenetics, sometimes in a biased manner, select topics to study based upon issues that are fundamentally socio-political and socio-economic rather than biological. Hence, both racism and nationalism have been integral ideological tenets in the history of Western Europe. These ideologies cannot be separated from the rest of the history of Western Europe, namely colonialism, capitalism, and personal prejudice. In truth then racism can only be studied socio-historically rather than biologically.

The biased initial theoretical assumption that everyone belongs to a particular racial classification is flawed ("either/or") thinking. Indeed, the study of race has taken on the "blind-alley" approach of socio-political propaganda. Europeans nationalized and racially oriented the world in order to exploit the world. Now this negative orientation dominates intragroup, intergroup, and international relations. More importantly, racialism in powerful countries tends to be forced upon less powerful countries. Historically then one can demonstrate that Europeans did indeed invent racism and culturally imposed it upon the rest of the world. Ideas about both nation-statehood and social class have their parallels in the race concept.

Culture is the carrier of language. Thus, language development is also socialization into a culture, a particular worldview. Language expresses ideas, concepts, constructs, and above all values. Therefore, in assimilating a language one inherits the symbols, ideologies, and values expressed by that culture. To adopt another group's language is invariably to adopt their mindset. Language development indeed is more than a communication tool.

This is why English has become the universal language of the world community; the English language has been used as a tool to promulgate white supremacy. Traditionally language was viewed as the primary research tool in the acquisition of a PhD degree. In recent times this notion has been replaced with the notion of statistics as a language, and therefore the only necessary research tool. Why? The implication is clear: because there are lies, damn lies, and how to lie with statistics. Therefore, if a research report is not predicated upon the English language, it obviously cannot arrive at any valid empirical conclusions.

To be sure, the logic of Western societies ("either/or") and the built-in assumptions in the scientific method automatically bias research conclusions in the direction of validating Western culture and therefore white supremacy. Even if one arrives at different conclusions, how can they be validated? Therefore, the key to understanding any definitional system is understanding its built-in theoretical assumptions, because the assumptions will dictate the character of the conclusions. How else can one explain the social fact that whites intellectually accept the principle of relativism but emotionally cling to absolutism in the form of white supremacy?

At best, too many whites are schizophrenic. In other words, the only absolute in the world community is whiteness. Even God is not an absolute among some whites, because an absolute requires 100 percent consensus.

There has never been a problem with getting consensus among whites on the issue of their supremacy. Unlike non-whiteness, whatever else whiteness is, it is viewed foremost as a divine state of being. Non-whiteness is viewed as divine error or biological error. So blackness, specifically, is a biological accident and therefore a condition that an individual needs to be liberated from.

Western cultures are entrenched in these socio-political ideas. One example is the symbol of the white robe. Historically, society has been divided into two domains: church (sacred) and state (secular). In the sacred domain, the minister represents God and therefore is privileged to wear the white robe. In the secular domain, the medical doctor represents God and also wears the white robe. (Notably, in the academic professions the robes are traditionally dark colors.)

Blackness is the color of sin, death, and evil in European thought. Enemies of the royal knights were always black. Even institutional Christianity utilized this commonly held relationship of blackness to evil. Europeans personified the notion of a physical devil, as opposed to a spiritual one. Why? In order to justify their exploitation of non-white people. Thus, whites, in the name of civilization, industrialization (the development of science and technology), and above all institutional Christianization, have created an evil world. Long before Europeans had physical contact with blacks and browns, their minds were full of distortions and prior assumptions about life.

Thus, prior to the eighteenth century, there were no ideas about racial classifications as meaningful categories. Europeans integrated existing biological theories and social theories about race in order to justify European expansion, colonialism, and chattel slavery. In order to perpetuate rugged individualism as the basis for human existence, Europeans had to develop a definitional system that perpetuated an order/model of (1) social change and (2) both intellectual and political conservatism (i.e., lies). But no lie can live forever.

Europeans have been driven by the dual spirit of adventure and control. Whites have always been unhappy wherever they were and therefore invariably always sought to go somewhere else, whether it was to America, Africa, or the moon. Who and what are whites running from? Obviously, whites are running from themselves. What is truly driving them is a lack of self-acceptance. To be sure, wherever individuals journey, they must take themselves along. It's not the physical environment but the character of the individual that gives meaning to life. The mind creates the environment and not vice versa.

Indeed, nationalism was based on racial and cultural homogeneity as an ideal. European nationalistic struggles have all but leveled the "mighty continent" to virtually no continent at all. This explains the migration and immigration of European nationals and white ethnics to America. Whites have not been able to live in "peace and harmony" among themselves because of their self-imposed insecurities. In other words, whites have projected onto non-whites what essentially is their own problem.

Before whites could exploit low self-esteem (insecurity) in non-whites the problem first had to exist in themselves. (The obsession of whites with suntanning as a status symbol is profoundly indicative of this social fact.) Whites went searching for non-whites because they didn't like themselves. This also explains why non-whites didn't go searching for whites.

To perpetuate an order/model of social change, whites elevated the Christian Bible as the authority over life for all the wrong reasons (i.e., selfishness). Yet today many whites do not subscribe to the Bible as the authority over their own personal lives. Whites wanted the Bible to be viewed as a dead, static document rather than a living, spiritual document.

Indeed, institutionalized Christianity has worked well for whites. By making the Bible static, unscientific, and unhistorical in character, the end result is individualism rather than human interdependence. That is, the Bible has become the basis for divisiveness (denominationalism) rather than unity in the human community.

Moreover, if a social system only allows for orderly (controlled) social change, then the inventors of that system will always have control over the system. Dr. Oscar Criner of Texas Southern University alludes to this order/model of social change as the "P-system":

- Protocol: institutionalized status differentiation
- Precedence: being the first, setting the standards (superiority)
- Procedures: order and authority
- Precision: regimentation and exact repetition
- Proof: logic and conclusive conclusions

Given the propositions mentioned earlier, one could argue that racial supremacy as an ideology is more likely to be found in Western cultures than non-Western cultures. It is also true that, in Europe as well as America, whites are obsessed with the P-system.

White supremacy invariably undermines social democracy and equality of opportunity. Conservative thought in Western cultures is based on six canons: (1) divine intent rules the universe, (2) tradition must be respected, (3) in civilized societies, order in the form of social classification is inevitable, (4) hero-worship is a strong value,

(5) discrimination (i.e., siphoning out individuals of no value) is an imperative, and (6) theological dogmatism is the rule.

The social history of whites is replete with the socio-psychological projections of their own mental insecurities, incompetency, inadequacies, and above all their human failures. The socio-political nationalistic struggles of whites in Europe forced them into formulating policies based upon theories about their historical origin. What we perceive as reality is determined by our self-consciousness—that is, our mind thinking about itself. Whites therefore institutionalized mental self-deceit, and as a result they continually come to erroneous conclusions about the nature of reality. Whites indeed are more victimized than non-whites by the notion of white supremacy because they started to believe their own lie.

The paradox of white supremacy dichotomized human existence into two levels: (1) physical and (2) spiritual. In other words, white supremacy triggered the negative action/reaction of institutionalizing matter over mind. This in turn makes it virtually impossible for whites to participate in being (ontology), or to experience the ground of their own spiritual existence. Individuals need communion with others (relatedness) and creative expression or else they become unconscious (dead) to the creative possibilities of human existence. White supremacy stifles spiritual creativity. Again, like the caterpillar in *Alice in Wonderland*, white supremacy seeks to give meaning to something that has no meaning.

The insanity of white supremacy has filtered into the Jewish affirmation of "the Chosen Ones" and has reached its barbaric apex in Hitlerism. Without a doubt, Hitler raised the question of "How white is white enough?" Racial superiority then has been the basis for socio-political actions of the most heinous nature. Indeed, history warns us of playing with extremes, just as we warn children not to play with fire.

Yet here is the human paradox: if individuals think about others first, they will learn how to become selfish. But if individuals think about self first, they will always operate from their strengths, they will not allow others to play upon their weaknesses, and they will therefore become generous.

"Having eyes ye see not, and having ears ye hear not, and do you not remember."

—Mark 8:18

BIBLIOGRAPHY

M. Banton and J. Harwood. *The Race Concept.* New York: Praeger Publishers, 1975.

R. Blauner. *Racial Oppression in America.* New York: Harper & Row Publishers, 1972.

A. Montagu. *Race and I.Q.* London: Oxford University Press, 1975.

W. J. Wilson. *Power, Racism, and Privilege.* New York: Free Press, 1976.

15 AFFIRMATIVE ACTION: METHOD OR IDEOLOGY?

Professional educators and social scientists in American society have naively assumed that the goal of both the socio-political-economic system and the educational system is the maximization of every individual's talents. This notion is consistent with the classical view of mass education as a force for personal and societal liberation. Indeed, social democracy is for an informed, intelligent citizenry. The dominant theme in educational philosophy is the meritocratic ideal—that is, the notion that the most talented and qualified individuals rise to and achieve educational and occupational success.

In a meritocratic system, the overriding assumption is free will—the idea that an individual is limited only by desire, intelligence, the motivation to achieve, and above all human willpower. These notions are the cornerstone of the American dream. Therefore, the notions of mass education and the "melting pot" theory are highly consistent with the image maker's ideal of "rags to riches." Thus, individuals who do not achieve educational and occupational success have only themselves to blame (the "blame the victim" theory).

Unfortunately, the American dream has become, in some instances, social justification for structural social inequalities. For many, the American dream is a dream deferred, and for too many, a total nightmare. The existence of a seemingly permanent underclass is a social testament to this fact, because at least 20 percent of America's population at any given time lives in poverty. It is the denial of the American dream to a large segment of Americans that has engendered the debate over affirmative action and so-called reverse discrimination: the method versus the ideology.

As with the 1954 Supreme Court desegregation decision, reactionary cultural elites are clouding the issue by overemphasizing methods, confusing methods with ideology as though they are one and the same. Initially, affirmative action was viewed as a method to remedy the historical victimization of blacks by American society. Without a doubt, blacks are denied equal access to developmental opportunities. Shifting the debate from the methods by which the society remedies structural inequality to the ideology about discrimination allows whites to view themselves as the victims of discrimination rather than the perpetrators of discrimination. To be sure, no one is in favor of "self-inflicting" discrimination, but if the other fellow is discriminated against, that's alright—especially if from such discriminatory processes one derives psychological and material benefits.

Had whites, as a social group, been as zealous in their defense of the integrity of the Constitution and the human rights of others as they have been to scream reverse discrimination, there would never have been a slave stratification system, nor would institutional racism continue to exist in the twenty-first century. Indeed, the sins of parents are always visited upon their children and future generations. Sin is a spiritual as well as social concept that implies accountability in terms of social cost. For indeed chickens always come home to roost. The price tag on righteousness is high, but the price tag on unrighteousness is higher. Without some notion of social justice, there could be no such animal as a civilized society.

The notion of affirmative action is conceptually similar to the issue of bussing. Both raise serious questions about the role and function of schooling. The question is how best to educate individuals. Neither the notion of affirmative action nor bussing is ideological, but rather they are artificial methods designed to create an integrated society. The goal of public schooling was never social democracy, and because democracy was not its goal, schooling has no goal. After all, schools are better at educating middle-class individuals than poor individuals.

Educational institutions perpetuate unequal access to developmental opportunities. Knowledge is a source of power. Schools colonize knowledge rather than maximize self-actualization, self-realization, and self-consciousness. Schools flunk the products (students) and not the producers (teachers and administrators), and of course this social fact in and of itself indicates the unstated goal of education: schools are organizationally designed to create elitism rather than social democracy. This is why a degree has become the single most important certification for getting a job, and why there is no relationship between the requirements to obtain the degree and performance requirements for the job.

But, more importantly, because schooling is a way to become credentialed, intelligence and aptitude tests are treated as objective indicators of intelligence and ability. Intelligence tests, by and large, have become culturally biased political screening devices. More often than not, intelligence tests only measure how well individuals can take tests, not the actual intelligence of the individual.

Schooling is designed as a holding process for the economic system, in many instances, to keep individuals out of the job market. As a society, we have a declining industrial job base. There are not enough jobs for everyone who is able and willing to work. It is also a well-known social fact that structurally the social system cannot create a job for every American. Society's definition of full employment (3 to 5 percent of the work population out of work) is indicative of this fact. This is why the Humphrey-Hawkins Full Employment Act (zero-based employment) did not pass in Congress.

This compounds the problem of affirmative action (blacks obtaining jobs because they are black, not because of qualifications), especially when whites view it as reverse discrimination. After all, whites understand this social phenomenon more so than anyone else because traditionally the first qualification of almost any job was to be white.

Because the culture and value orientations of schools reflect the ideology of the upper class (time equals money), schools are the result of elitist rule. Without a doubt, the goal of the ruling class is to restrict access to knowledge, professional credentials, and above all the "false god" of money. American society is over credentialed and over professionalized, but under humanized. Any society that uses materialism as a means to create artificial inequality is an incompetent, disoriented society. When a society arbitrarily creates competition and artificial scarcities between individuals, then social conflict defines human interaction. A democratic society should be humane enough to allow individuals to foster internal self-competition rather than external competition. That is, the individual maximizes his talents when he competes within himself, and consequently society derives the highest benefits. Thus education is a social process that dehumanizes because it has a negative purpose.

Negativism is not a purpose. Educational institutions at every level in American society are in serious trouble because they have become static, chaotic, intolerant, authoritarian, and above all averse to social change. The nature of learning (i.e., openness) requires social democracy, and educational institutions are not social democracies but authoritarian social systems. In fact, an individual's education usually gets in the way of his or her learning, because oftentimes the structure of schooling is an impediment to learning. This is how education has become the power tool of cultural elitism in American society, rather than social democracy.

Institutional racism is a societal problem, and American society is seeking to resolve this societal problem by using its weakest institution: public schools. This in and of itself presents a serious problem because the American educational system is an impediment to social justice (i.e., equality of opportunity). One can't successfully employ a problem to resolve a problem. We can't expect schools to purge themselves of both externally and internally imposed inequalities. Educational institutions need a value overhaul and a basic restructuring both in kind and degree. Inequality is a structural, societal economic problem. The question of how best to eradicate economic inequality poses other questions concerning the issue of social justice. The external pressure exerted on public schools to create fairness/equality of outcome and equality of opportunity is significant. At the same time, it should be noted that schools cannot create equality of outcome, but they can create equality of access (opportunity).

The confusion over affirmative action ought to cause professional educators and social scientists to do some serious soul searching. In particular, how much of the educational process is designed to develop skills and knowledge, and how much of it is designed as a social labeling process to restrict access to valued resources?

At any given time in American society, almost 100 million Americans are in public schools, colleges, and universities. What are they learning? Is it knowledge and understanding, truth and wisdom? Or are these individuals being tracked by society into certain socio-political-economic roles? Schooling has been designed as a social process to perpetuate a white-male-dominated authoritarian power structure (elitism). Or is it simply social engineering? Either way, education has been designed to perpetuate racism and sexism, not to create equality of opportunity and equality of outcome. Ethnically "tanned" minorities, because of past cultural and environmental inequalities, can't be concerned solely with opportunity itself, but with the meaning of opportunity.

How to societally correct institutional racism and sexism is a socio-political question. The question is which segment of society pays, not how minorities should become responsible productive citizens. Another way to frame the question is, does society continually victimize the victims? Or does society adjust its institutional structure to include those it has deliberately excluded? This was the issue the Supreme Court had to address in its deliberations in the Bakke case.

Dan Lacy, in his book *The White Use of Blacks in America*, states the problem precisely:

> To meet what the dominant whites thought were their needs they had to create a labor force that was not free to share in the abundance of land or compete for the skill job openings in industry, that did not share in the Declaration's equality of all men or participate in the addressee's government by the people, that was denied the determination of one's own destiny that America meant to its other children. To achieve this goal required a vigorous and coherent public policy made up of laws, of folkways, of diligently implanted attitudes. It required the participation of the State, the Churches, the Schools, the press and society generally. The smooth collaboration of governmental, institutional, and private action is without parallel in our history. We assembled and maintained that labor force large, productive, and consuming only at the margins of subsistence—through all the kaleidoscopic changes of our

history: through the colonial period, through the revolution and independence, through the tidal sweep to the Pacific, through the Civil War and Reconstruction, through the creation of vast cities, and overwhelming industries of modern America. In the last generation our goals have changed. The mindless machine can do the work of the unskilled and the landowners once desperately dependent on black labor now turn from it in indifference. The unskilled or semi-skilled labor force that was once a necessity is now an embarrassment, unusable in our economy.[8]

It suits America now, in the twenty-first century, to "discredit" that segment of society that is unusable and unproductive in our economy, and which it fears. If you want to destroy a social group, attack the institution that is seen as the basis of society (family) and decry that there are external, independent causal dynamics that account for its social disorganization or economic impoverishment. Institutional racism is a fundamental principle of American society, not an aberration of it. That is, race and racism are not figments of demented imaginations but are the baseline of American culture, economics, education, and politics. Of course, whites who have been screaming that blacks should stop yelling racism ought to take their own advice and stop screaming reverse discrimination. The socio-political concept of race becomes extremely important when a society infers a causal relationship between physical attributes and cultural behavior.

The propagandist research of Moynihan, Jensen, and Jencks does not serve as an intellectual framework to explain away the social fact of white institutional and cultural racism. Again, one question comes to mind: if whites are superior in native intelligence, why did they institutionalize inequality (privilege)? The natural thing to do would

---

8   Dan Lacy, *The White Use of Blacks in America* (McGraw-Hill, 1972), pp. 4-5.

have been to create an open-ended social system that would allow for open-ended competition for "scarce" valued resources (based on the idea of natural selection and survival of the fittest). Obviously, the American social system is not totally an open-ended competitive system. Thus, because of this "power differential," the larger dominant white culture structures institutional arrangements that cause prophecies to become self-fulfilling.

Therefore, the corruption of whites is by and large a function of the power differential between whites and blacks, not skin color. Human nature is what it is. Hence, if the social structure is responsible for the existence of poverty and inequality, then how rewards are apportioned and allocated must be altered, and concomitantly, institutions and the values upon which they rest must be radically impacted. Within this context then, it was American society and the meaning of social democracy that was on trial in the Bakke case.

Social justice for whites in American society has always been a universal assumption. Thus, given the notion of meritocracy, special-purpose structures and processes can always be attacked as unnecessary, using the melting pot theory and more recently the notion of "crossover." To be sure then, whites have posited affirmative action as an ideology rather than a methodology. The ideology of affirmative action focuses on the idea that blacks and browns are getting jobs they are allegedly not qualified to hold. Thus affirmative action as an ideology means white mercy rather than real social justice. The Supreme Court in the Bakke decision simply demonstrated that black freedom is not housed in white institutional structures and legal processes; black freedom is housed in self-initiatives.

Historically, blacks have been viewed as the property of white America and therefore had no civil rights. The right to work for freedom has not always been a universal assumption in American society. For example, the Rodney King verdict and its horrible social aftermath (riots) provide another example of blacks being viewed as property, and of course the end result was that blacks demonstrated a total disrespect for property rights. Indeed property cannot value property; only human beings value property. This is why Rodney King, after being brutalized by the police, could say, "Can't we all just get along?"

As a society, we must institute the societal concept of economic opportunity and dispense with the sideshow of affirmative action.

16 A PHILOSOPHICAL ANALYSIS OF DEMOCRACY, POWER, LEADERSHIP, AND COMMITMENT IN AMERICAN SOCIETY

Power in modern industrial societies is viewed as a zero-sum-game—that is, you either have power or you do not. Obviously, power is not that one-dimensional in character. Power indeed manifests itself in two dimensions: leadership and followership. Individuals cannot be good leaders, in my opinion, unless they have been good followers. Power as a social concept then can only be understood in a social collective. Unfortunately, many who aspire to become leaders view power as only leadership and in effect become leaders of leaderless groups. In other words, one cannot lead unless another is willing to intelligently and intellectually follow. Thus social democracy requires both an intelligent leadership as well as an intelligent followership. To be sure, social democracy is for a spiritually enlightened society.

All individuals possess unique talents that in turn become potential motivating forces for leadership. Therefore, every individual has a power source (uniqueness) and is a potential leader or follower in every recurrent social situation. However, an individual must have a "social-political eye" for knowing when to seek to play which social role. This timing factor requires the ability to objectively assess one's own strengths and weaknesses.

Because an individual is essentially a learner, the greatest source of power in society is individual uniqueness. Shared knowledge is equally important. Yet knowledge in American society is colonized and privileged by such social factors as race, ethnicity, sex, social class, academic degrees, regionalism, and so on. Hence, the tragedy of the human condition is not that individuals might have only one talent, but that society does not allow the individual to creatively realize and use his one talent. Difference in American society invariably becomes a basis for the inequality of opportunity (discrimination). But real strength comes out of difference, not artificial and arbitrary mechanical sameness. Sadly, American society is held together by mechanical sameness rather than spiritual enlightenment and moral togetherness.

A society's power comes out of the ability of individuals and society to integrate ideas, in order to integrate cultures, social processes, social systems, and above all subcultures. Ideas rule the universe. It is ideas that affect human behavior and social structures. For example, religion, like politics, is about ideas, and therefore religion and politics cannot be ideologically compartmentalized. Men are political *and* religious—not either/or, but *and*. Religion and politics are interdependent social processes of learning how to live in relationship to the material world, given that we are biological and spiritual beings. Thus, on the one hand, politics in American society has not been about the competition of ideas and a quest for truth, but rather the perpetuation of personal privilege (re-election). Indeed, few politicians seek to establish themselves as statesmen insofar as a politician thinks of the next election and a statesman thinks of the next generation(s). On the other hand, there is relatively little difference between American values (the Constitution) and religious values (the gospel of Jesus).

Power is not necessarily material in character (i.e., in the form of guns, force, money, and so on). Material power is only a resource in the "bag of power," alongside love, trust, and above all human will. The Vietnam War taught us this lesson. Indeed, the will of the Vietnamese was stronger in might than American militarism. Without a doubt, material power cannot be used to control the contingencies of the future. The future belongs to God; men do not control all of the variables or have the ability to manipulate all of the variables. The desire of individuals to act as though they were gods always causes them to use material power to cut off spiritual power (knowledge and human will).

Power then is the ability of individuals to use human and non-human resources to create the highest good, not create evil or negativism. Power must never be viewed as an end, but rather as a means to an end. For when power is the end-all, social pathology ensues. The most profound modern (yet timeless) example of power as social pathology (or spiritual sickness) is Watergate. Because the Nixon "demolition crew" viewed power as an end in and of itself, its uses could only be negativism—to destroy or veto. The question is, destroy what?

Again, social democracy is for an intellectually enlightened and spiritually intelligent people, because social democracy requires intelligent social participation. John Dewey states the problem precisely:

Democracy is much broader than a special political form, a method of conducting a government, of making laws, and carrying on governmental administration by means of popular suffrage and elected officers. It is that, of course, but it is something broader and deeper than that. The political and governmental phase of democracy is a means, the best means so far found, for realizing ends that lie in the domain of human relationships and the development of human personality. It is, as we often say, though perhaps without appreciating all that is involved in the saying, a way of life, social and individual. The keynote to democracy as a way of life may be expressed, it seems to me, as the necessity for participation of every mature human being as individuals . . . .

Democratic political forms are simply the best means that human wit has devised up to a special time in history. But they rest back upon the idea that no man or limited set of men is wise enough or good enough to rule others without their consent.

Social democracy is about human resource development and spiritual values. Institutional racism and sexism undermine democratic processes. Thus, in a culturally racist-oriented society, non-whites cannot lead whites. To be sure then, the only model of leadership and authority in American society is white leadership, and the only model of cultural oppression is non-white oppression. Therefore, only whites can lead whites, and the only blacks who can lead blacks are the ones whites legitimate as leaders—which in effect means the lack of accountability of leadership in American society. In other words, racism undermines leadership accountability both for blacks as well as whites. Racism precludes a black leadership model; it only allows for a black "follower" model. Institutional racism and sexism are processes solely designed to perpetuate a white-male-dominated authoritarian power structure (elitism), not social democracy.

Democracy must invariably foster a spiritual culture and spiritual internal values rather than secular (external materialistic) values. Why? An external value system fosters value-commitment to materialism rather than human resources development. Social processes in a democracy must be designed to create democratic personalities rather than authoritarian personalities. To be sure, individuals must be educated toward a democratic state of being, a way of life that embraces totally the concept of egalitarianism.

> Democracy is often associated in our minds with freedom of action, and, as a consequence, we forget the importance of freed intelligence which is necessary to direct freedom of action . . . . Unless freedom of individual action has intelligence and informed conviction back of it, its manifestation is almost sure to result in confusion and disorder. If individuals are not free to develop, society is deprived of what they might contribute.[9]

Unfortunately, in American society economic processes motivate all social processes. This in turn has produced a business society that is chaotic and over-materialistic in its cultural orientations. Indeed, a value commitment to materialism invariably undermines the idealized goals of social democracy. Americans love things and exploit people. Because Americans love things more than people, we have no basis for universal community and nation-statehood. That is, an abiding respect for the sanctity of human life is the *only* basis for human community. Obviously, the astounding rates of crimes against persons are symbolic of our disdain for human life, and more importantly our love of material artifacts.

Social democracy is about cooperative spiritual interaction, not negative individualistic competition over artificially contrived materialistic scarcities. Material values create social isolationism rather than a creative tension between individual survival and collectivistic interaction. When individuals value material goodies in and of themselves, there will never

---

9   John Dewey, "The Ethos of a Democratic Society," in Harold J. Carter, ed., *The Intellectual Foundation of American Education* (New York: Pitman Publishing Company, 1965), pp. 17-18.

be enough to go around. Hence, individualistic competition, greed, envy, and jealousy will always stand as obstacles to generous sharing. Democracy dictates notions about shared leadership, shared power, and above all shared commitments and responsibilities.

The notion of formal schooling ought to fully embrace the democratic ethos. That is, schooling ought to epitomize the democratic ethos in action. Naturally, the types of educational strategies and methods that are employed to create learning environments are of strategic importance. Schooling in a democratic society dictates a distinctive systematic organizational form.

The value orientation of schooling must reflect the idealized values of the democratic ethos, and the idealized goal of American education must be participatory democracy. Thus, schooling in a society with democratic aspirations must reflect value commitments that foster the following philosophical notions: collective interaction, interdependence, openness, flexibility, humaneness, cultural expansion, innovativeness, and so on.

Schooling must also generate priorities that foster the idealized goals of social democracy. For life is about setting priorities—that is, deciding where to place one's ultimate trust. Yet many of those who are to be served by schooling are systematically isolated from effective social participation in the democratic process. Contrary to popular expectations, our current system of schooling fosters the business ethos rather than the democratic ethos. In fact, the organization of schools reflects the business model of bureaucratic organization. Schools are authoritarian structures rather than social democracies. We educate individuals in American society just like we grow mushrooms—keep them in the dark and feed them a lot of manure.

We have failed to realize the idealized goals of democracy because we have failed to create the kind of distinctive educational processes that are indeed inherent to the formation of a democratic state. Unfortunately, public school social disorganization is only symbolic of the undemocratic character of schooling. It is only through constant social learning that the idealized values sought by social democracy will inspire individuals to travel the high roads rather than the low roads.

Where there is democracy, there is hope.

Where there is hope, there is love.

Where there is love, there is peace.

Where there is peace, there is God.

Where there is God, there is no need!

The corporate business ethos in American society has altered all social relationships into object relationships. Americans view each other in terms of dollar signs to be exploited. This in turn has produced a loss of consciousness about the real meaning of social democracy. In fact, the corporate business ethos (the structures of industrial society) has produced the colonization of private life in American society, in that workers value themselves as most individuals value all material artifacts—by market price. Indeed, price and quality have become synonymous. To be sure, in a corporate business ethos, individual worth is measured solely by how much "labor" he or she will bring into the market system. Materialism creates human exploitation like a dairy farmer who consistently milks his cows but seldom feeds them.

Democracy, above all, values the human personality in and of itself. Democracy is not "ad-hocracy" but rather systematic methodological processes that are designed to maximize egalitarianism—that is, equal access to valued resources and opportunities. Many political leaders in American society are obsessed with personal privileges rather than a burning desire to establish a healthy democratic society, or fostering principles of how best to achieve social democracy. Authoritarianism invariably causes individuals to confuse ideology and methodology. Without a doubt, individuals must be educated in the niceties of the style of democratic leadership.

Authoritarianism has both American political and educational processes on a treadmill that is on dead center and going nowhere. Both educational and political institutions in American society have boxed themselves in to a static, elitist value orientation. Education, just like politics in American society, is more about racism, sexism, and classism than social democracy.

The creative possibilities of social democracy as a way of life demand that we embrace social processes within governmental organization—as well as in our personal relationships—that facilitate the realization of the idealized goals of the democratic ethos.

If social democracy is to be revitalized, then Americans must (a) restructure educational processes to symbolize the idealized values of the democracy and its spiritual ethos, (b) limit corporate power by insisting on a more competitive free marketplace, as well as broader control over corporate power by agencies external to corporations, and (c) institutionalize collective responsibility for the exercise of social power and political power. Indeed, capitalism has become anti-democratic, and education has become anti-learning.

17 THE TWENTY-FIRST-CENTURY CIVIL WAR: UPSIDE DOWN

When the Civil War ended and President Abraham Lincoln initiated the Reconstruction process, everyone knew that a price would have to be levied upon the South for its egregious transgressions. Question: was a true price levied for the magnitude of pain, suffering, destruction, and death? This question must be asked because seemingly no spiritual/moral lessons were learned: a nation divided against itself cannot stand. While the president and Congress argued for about two years (1865-1867) over who would control the Reconstruction process, the South instituted the same governmental system they had prior to the Civil War. Instead of slave codes, the South instituted black codes.

President Lincoln was assassinated and succeeded by Andrew Johnson. President Andrew Johnson was the worst president in history for blacks because he basically felt that blacks should not be free. President Johnson vetoed the Fourteenth Amendment, the Civil Rights Act of 1866, and all other positive legislation. In fact, President Johnson did absolutely nothing to improve the plight of black Americans.

In 1867, with the passage of the Reconstruction Act, Congress seized control of the Reconstruction process. Because of the Reconstruction Act, federal troops were sent to the South to protect blacks and enforce the Fourteenth Amendment. During this ten-year period of Reconstruction, blacks received the right to vote, elected blacks to public office, built educational institutions, and established churches and other civic/voluntary associations. While these were significant gains, Reconstruction was in fact a failure because blacks were never given the forty acres and a mule (in other words, economic restitution). It has been said that Lincoln freed the slaves, but because blacks did not receive land, although they may have been free physically, they were still economic slaves.

To make matters worse, in 1872 large numbers of Republicans turned away from promoting the rights of blacks and embraced big corporate business. When you couple these historical facts with the election of Rutherford B. Hayes to the office of the presidency in 1877, and his decision to remove federal troops from the South, any gains that blacks made during Reconstruction were wiped out in the twinkling of an eye. President Hayes's decision to remove federal troops gave rise to the sharecropping system and Jim Crowism, which created a system of separate but unequal facilities. Of course, this system was aided and abetted by lynching, disenfranchisement, and above all unjust laws coupled with brutal enforcement.

The South, having lost its greatest commodity (free slave labor) and counting the cost, was willing to preserve its glorious lifestyle at any price and would not pay restitution. In the capital city of Jackson, Mississippi, government leaders commissioned a cornerstone on city hall that reads: "built by slave labor in 1846-47; material costs $7,505.58." The Southern lifestyle based upon slave labor was even romanticized in the movie *Gone with the Wind*, in which Ashley states that one day his intentions are to free his slaves. But we know this was motion picture spin to give the perception of white male integrity. That "one day" would never become a reality. Fast forward to today: white males in the 2013 Virginia governor's race primarily voted for the Republican candidate, while white females voted strongly for the Democratic candidate. Why? The twenty-first-century civil war is about social class distinction (economic structure/distribution), and race/ethnicity is only an underlying issue.

Modern history has proved that there was one Southern white man, President Lyndon Baines Johnson (LBJ), who had enough spiritual and intellectual integrity to seek to give liberty to individuals caught up in the Jim Crow system of the South by giving them the civil rights already promised by the Constitution. Of course, there were other whites who felt the same way, and they convinced still other whites, who finally came along kicking and screaming. Protecting anyone's civil rights should never have been a problem, given the spiritual nature of the US Constitution, but it became a problem for blacks because of whites' desire for free labor and a problem for white women because many white men did not want to follow the commonsense principle of one vote per person. Unfortunately, there are too many Americans in the twenty-first century who find it easy to live with spiritual/moral constitutional contradictions in order to maximize vulgar economic advantages. In fact, because of demographic changes, white males are slowing becoming politically extinct and are now doubling down on the "greed factor" in such an economically vulgar fashion that it is creating a political gender rift between white men and white women.

On the one hand, what LBJ did to improve the plight of blacks is not properly celebrated and appreciated in the black community. This is primarily true because of the Vietnam War and the disproportionate number of blacks who died in Vietnam. On the other hand, whites too are trying very hard to forget his contribution, because President Lyndon B. Johnson was a white Southerner who had an epiphany that all Americans should enjoy being American. Apparently many white males cannot forgive President Johnson and at the same time hold themselves accountable for the economic cost of their inhumanity to blacks as well as to themselves for institutional racism.

Throughout American history, in my humble opinion, there have been only two presidents who were able to exercise the spiritual creative power of the executive branch of government to include all Americans: Franklin D. Roosevelt and Lyndon B. Johnson. These two presidents leveled the playing field for all Americans more so than any other presidents.

Reflecting back on the nineteenth-century ruling class economic structure, in conjunction with the political ruling class and institutional racism, it seems as though society has not learned the lessons of the past and is destined to repeat its sins. Some Southern white males and Northern white male sympathizers plotted the assassination of Lincoln in order to keep the Union divided (along the Mason-Dixon Line) because Lincoln was a stabilizing factor for a "just" society. Vice President Andrew Johnson was a white male scoundrel who wanted to have the "good ole days relived," and of course not have the South pay for the sins of the past through restitution (forty acres and a mule). This conspiracy convinced John Wilkes Booth to assassinate President Lincoln because they knew that Vice President Andrew Johnson was a "Southern sympathizer." However, it was President Rutherford B. Hayes who removed Union troops from the South and turned the "dogs" loose on defenseless blacks, with the black codes.

President Lincoln's Reconstruction program had promised forty acres and a mule to all slave families as restitution (for work already done). Lincoln sincerely believed that no individual should work without receiving the benefits of his own labor. But blacks never received the promised restitution of forty acres and a mule; instead they received a sharecropping system called the "company store." Therefore, blacks never received a fair share of the crops they produced.

The recent civil rights case of black farmers against the federal government is a classic example of the nature of the economic injustice. The company store simply kept economic slavery alive and well. With the assassination of President Lincoln, the South returned to business as usual (i.e., a plantation mentality), instituting the black codes and organizing the night riders, the White Citizen Council, and above all the Ku Klux Klan (KKK) in order to murder and continue to intimidate blacks and white sympathizers.

Blacks have always known that the role of law enforcement was to protect white males and their property rights. The case of *Plessy v. Ferguson* is the classic example that preserved this notion. To a large degree, white women were considered as property as well, and their struggle for freedom was basically the same as that of blacks, eventually coming through the same mechanism: the Commerce Department.

In a society that is supposedly based upon meritocracy, why have only white males historically had all of the economic advantages and opportunities, while at the same time legal restrictions have been levied on all other males—especially black males? Institutional racism and gender discrimination are inextricably tied together in American culture. White males want black men to apologize for being black. But God creates human beings. Individuals do not create themselves or create other human beings. Black men should not have to apologize if God created them with the mental and physical ability to walk and chew gum at the same time. This state of affairs explains why one-eighth black blood, regardless of skin tone or other physical characteristics, historically defined the status of blackness. This was done simply to protect property rights inheritance. Even the concept of illegitimacy to a large degree was created to protect white male property rights.

The Civil War was not primarily about freeing slaves but preserving the "Union" and maintaining the economic structure of Southern society (i.e., white male dominance). Prior to the Civil War, blacks numbered approximately 25 percent of the population. Today blacks number about 12 percent of the population. One of the main reasons for the black population decline was European immigration in order to dilute the population impact of blacks. The other reason was the extreme physical violence (often murder) and mental violence exacted on blacks, especially black men. Similar methods were used against American Indians, which resulted in their virtual extinction. A classic modern version of such violence was the Emmett Till case of Mississippi, in which a fourteen-year-old black male from Chicago whistled at a white female, and he was brutalized and then hanged. The Emmett Till case is just one of many such incidents.

The game plan of the South has not changed; it remains the same (cheap labor). From 1860 until the present day we have had a number of free-land initiatives that allowed European white males to immigrate to America with the promise of six hundred acres of land and cheap labor. This process was designed to ensure white male economic dominance.

In the twentieth century, white males instituted a modern form of self-enslavement called "illegal immigration," which in turn allowed Hispanics, especially Mexican nationals, to economically enslave themselves as domestic workers, migrant farm laborers, construction workers, and service industry workers. Unfortunately, the illegal immigration process has fueled an undercurrent of international resentment between the United States and Mexico. The Southwestern part of the United States was lost in a war against Mexico. Mexico lost two wars to the United States, and Mexican landowners lost the land

and everything else: to the victor go the spoils. This has fueled Mexican resentment to the *nth* degree.

Yet, after the Civil War, there was Reconstruction on the backs of freed blacks, not restitution. In short, Southern Reconstruction was initiated upon the backs of freed former slaves. Now America has an illegal immigration problem and a South American drug problem that white males know how to solve, but because of their economic advantages and unbridled greed, they do not have the will to do so. Everyone knows what's wrong with illegal immigration: what's wrong with it is that it's illegal.

In my humble opinion, illegal immigration was permitted to flourish in order to change the dynamics of the historical mental conflict and tension between white males and blacks due to institutional racism. The Emancipation Proclamation of 1863 supposedly freed blacks from slave labor, but even in modern times this has proved to be untrue. Illegal immigration was designed to shift the nature of the mental conflict to one between blacks and browns rather than blacks and whites. This strategy has proved to be spiritually, morally, and economically extremely costly because blacks, unlike some other ethnic groups, do not tend to hold grudges (i.e., resentment).

Mexican overlords, who number only 6 percent of the population, control 94 percent of the wealth in Mexico, and 94 percent of Mexico's population controls only 6 percent of the wealth. In America, "multinational gurus," who number 23 percent of the population, control 77 percent of the wealth. Even in Russia, the bastion of socialism, 180 individuals own 70 percent of the wealth of the nation. This process has created an upside-down economic structure where the rich get richer and the poor remain poor. All Americans face the same international threats but not the same domestic threats, because the extremely rich can minimize both their international and domestic threats.

Now we can examine how the twenty-first-century civil war that has been raging as an undercurrent in America (from the previous Civil War) intersects with the hijacking of the Republican Party. It is not by chance that the "ultra-extreme faction" of the Republican Party no longer refers to itself as the party of Lincoln, but the party of Ronald Reagan. The question is, what is the meaning of the Reagan Doctrine? Is it black dehumanization?

The election of Abraham Lincoln gave rise to extreme groups, especially the KKK and the White Citizen Council. The election of Barack Obama gave rise to "change," but it also has given rise to extreme groups like the Tea Party/Tree Party, or electronic lynching extremists. The real question is, why is there all this uncivil discourse in American politics? For example, an organized movement questions whether President Obama is an American citizen (the "birthers"), some question his Christianity, a congressman during the State of the Union address yelled "you lie" at the president, individuals bring guns to political meetings near where the president is speaking, and a hack unsophisticated politician with a limited understanding of national and international affairs becomes the leading spokesperson for a major political party. (More importantly, this hack politician has become extremely wealthy overnight.)

The Tea Party has taken the Reagan Doctrine to the *nth* degree, the uncivilized saying and doing of anything under the sun. Seemingly, the Reagan Doctrine made it fashionable to publicly demonize minorities. The Tea Party, in conjunction with the extreme right-wing faction of the Dixiecrat-Republican Party, has disrespected the executive branch of our governmental system simply because a "black family" resides in the White House.

Symbols motivate human behavior. The White House is called the White House for a reason. The White House was painted white for a reason. It was not an arbitrary act, even though a black man, namely

Benjamin Banneker, completed the engineering design for the White House. Yet, in the black designer's mind, he knew that it was not for him or his kind only because of his skin color. As of this writing, a black family resides in a governmental house that was built for whites only; too many white males cannot live with that reality, and of course American society is coming unglued. After all, "Mr. President" is a title reserved only for white males. The title "boy" is the appropriate reference for black men. In fact, one of America's leading conservative talk-show hosts refers to President Obama as "boy." Apparently, there is nothing in President Obama's past or present that morally discredits his presidential leadership in any way, and this social fact is disconcerting to many Americans. This has not been true of many of America's past presidents. (However, I must say that Habitat for Humanity speaks loud and profoundly clear for the spiritual/moral character of President James Earl Carter.)

The North has been weakened by the hijacking of the Republican Party by going along in order to get along. The Dixiecrats, with their open defiance of labor unions, have encouraged and guaranteed cheap labor for multinational corporations (the corporatization of America). For example, the industrial foundation of America's economy is the automobile industry, and now that base is steadily moving south and growing stronger because of non-union shops and cheap labor, and of course this in most instances limits black employment. This is not simply to imply that if blacks received their fair share of jobs this process would be justifiable.

Isn't it a strange twist that Republicans did not want to bail out the automobile industry? Could it simply be that the automobile industry in the South is primarily foreign, non-union, and highly profitable, while in the North it is primarily domestic and unionized? With this process, even migration patterns have reversed. In the North (the Rust Belt), industrial jobs are being outsourced overseas for cheap labor and

Northerners have lost the ability to provide for their families—and consequently we are witnessing the great Northern migration to the South. Now that white Northerners are migrating south for economic reasons, they must learn Southern attitudinal folkways and mores about how Southern whites treat minorities, especially blacks, and of course they become fast learners.

Southerners volunteer more frequently for military service, and consequently most military installations are housed in the South. Therefore, Republicans favor military spending for this economic reason (economic welfare for the rich and the South). This is the old "guns vs. butter" dichotomy, and of course the North receives no butter. In fact, the strategy of LBJ in passing civil rights/voting rights legislation was the open threat— which really was a promise—to remove all federal military installations from the South, because the South was living off the welfare of the federal government.

Wall Street is primarily a group of white males whose main interest is bottom-line economics (the greed factor). But money is neutral and has no value in and of itself, and certainly no intellectual capacity. The only value that money has is the value that individuals attach to it. If individuals attach inappropriate values to money, then they will tend to use money as fools, rather than as tools. If Wall Street executives (again, mostly white males) had to evaluate the capability of who could win the twenty-first century civil war, then their economic power would be guaranteed to support a Southern victory. The Midwest would join the South, and of course a number of the Western states would as well because they have already defeated themselves due to their doctrine of "go along in order to get along" so as to share power with the Dixiecrats.

The North has created a much better educational system than the South. Yet, because of emotional, economic, and ethnic prejudicial ignorance, the North has been manipulated into politically participating in its own economic suicide. To be sure, suicide is not an answer because suicide is a false choice. The North, out of self-centered economic and political interests rather than national interest, has brought itself to utter chaos. This process has given rise to a new South, which in turn is ready to receive the spoils of its inevitable victorious "rise again" philosophical approach. Of course, no physical shots have been fired this time, only economic and philosophical shots. Therefore, the South is winning the twenty-first-century civil war each and every day because of the war's nonviolent nature and the complete brainwashing of the North by Southerners and Southern sympathizers.

The real beginning of the twenty-first-century civil war was seeded in the passage of the Civil Rights Bill of 1964 and the Voting Rights Act of 1965, spearheaded by that courageous Southern white man, President Lyndon Baines Johnson. During the first Civil War, the Republican Party was primarily based in the North, and the Democratic Party was primarily based in the South. In 2014, the opposite is true: the Republican Party is primarily a Southern party, and there are virtually no Republicans to speak of in the Northeast. The question is, why?

After the Civil War, the South declared that it would rise again. In fact, in some Southern states the Confederate flag still flies over state capitols. The question is, rise against whom, and on whose back? The South would rise up against the Union—i.e., the federal government—therefore the federal government has become the problem for many right-wing conservatives. This is the current battlecry of the Tea Party: hatred of the federal government is the problem, not corporate greed or becoming "too big to fail." This is why some Republican Dixiecrat governors have openly talked about seceding from the Union. Southerners and Southern sympathizers have made it appear as though the federal government, especially the executive branch, is the source of all evil and social problems, even though white males primarily run the government. Of course, according to critics, the immoral/

evil economic business practices of Wall Street and multinational corporations have played little or no role in the economic decline of American society.

With no penalties being imposed for seceding from the Union and initiating the Civil War, the South has risen out of the ashes of Atlanta, Georgia—the symbol of the New South. The attributes that many white males who control the hierarchy of the economic structure of American society use to characterize blacks (laziness, shiftlessness, and ineptness) are more applicable to some white males. How else can one account for poverty among some white males? Perhaps because they want to be in charge but do not want to work and be accountable to all, only reap benefits from the labor of others.

It's strange that the designation of full employment by the federal government is when 3-4 percent of white males are unemployed and 10-12 percent of black males are unemployed. That percentage equates to millions of unemployed black men; how can they pay for ordinary preventable illnesses, let alone catastrophic illnesses? Obviously, they cannot. As Florida Congressman Alan Grayson stated, "Just die, quickly." This is the thinking of Southern Dixiecrats and unfortunately some Southern sympathizers. Again, Southern sympathizers are voting against their own best economic self-interests, especially in terms of unemployment, in order to "go along to get along" for the sake of sharing perceived power.

God gives us eyes to see, ears to hear, mouths to speak, hands to work with, strong backs to carry heavy loads, hearts to love and forgive our transgressors, and minds that enable all of the above to come to know white males for what they are and not what they want others to perceive them to be.

A *Times-Newsweek* magazine article in the mid-1970s listed ten things that white males fear the most. Topping the list was the fear of being poor—that is, of not having money. It is written that "the love of money is the root of all evil." America has written on its currency "in God we trust." It seems as though these are simply hollow words.

America and indeed the world community can learn a profound lesson from the Chilean miners. Thirty-three Chilean miners (thirty-three being a divine number) were trapped sixty-eight days a half mile under the earth, with only enough food to last two days. Yet under these adverse circumstances, the miners created a community under the reality of God, whereby equal is equal, not "more or less" equal. We know that all thirty-three survived, but more importantly we know why they survived. The first miner that was rescued declared: "I met God, and I met the devil, and God won." If America is to survive, God's reality must win, not the devil's. For after all, God gave Noah the rainbow sign: "no more water, but fire the next time."

18 THE DECLINE OF AMERICAN SOCIAL DEMOCRACY

Did the founding fathers really believe that all individuals were created equal? The answer is most likely an emphatic *no*. I seriously doubt that the founding fathers would have ever allowed slaves to vote. After all, even in the twenty-first century the sons of some former slave owners do not want the sons and daughters of former slaves to vote. America is seeking to spread democracy in the Middle East but at the same time is curtailing the cornerstone of democracy in America: voting rights.

The right to vote in a democratic society is a sacred right. The concept of one individual, one vote, is the cornerstone of social democracy. The recent, narrow, seemingly political decision of the US Supreme Court to strip the 1965 Voting Rights Act of key voting rights protections is to say the least democratically tragic. America should not accept these kinds of third-world political tactics, not now or ever. After almost four hundred years of chattel slavery, institutional racism, Jim Crowism, and lynchings by the KKK, blacks cannot sit idly by and observe their demise in the political process, after sacrificing and even dying for the sacred right to vote. In a democratic society, the right to vote is for everyone, not some.

It has been said that America is the greatest social democracy in the world community. Not so fast. More scrutiny is needed of ourselves and of others. The rampant moral corruption in our political system, at every level, needs self- examination, including the very essence of our economic engine, capitalism, and the idea of "too big to fail." After all, workers have rights, and their families are just as important as the families of business executives. Moving the political process in a one-dimensional direction is not a well-thought-out democratic idea, because this process leads to elections being bought and sold to the highest bidder. But, more importantly, it leads to a one-party political system called the corporate party. Of course, this leads to corporations wanting the federal government to pay them for creating jobs for workers, and they receive all the profits—while at the same time paying no taxes or minimal taxes. This is quite evident and most prevalent in Southern states. Large corporations claim they take all the risk; therefore they deserve all the profit. Not so fast. The American way is to use other people's money based upon an excellent business plan with very little collateral. Small businesses take more risks. Sadly, as it is, the desire is to regain control over the political process in order to control the economic system for the benefit of the super-rich. President Dwight Eisenhower called this dangerous state of affairs the "military-industrial complex."

Political systems define and attempt to implement policies deemed to be in the best interest of society in general. The form of the definition and the means of implementation have varied. The 1965 Voting Rights Act was a significant step toward involving "every"

American citizen in the political process and remedying past voting rights injustices. The Voting Rights Act was authored by President Lyndon B. Johnson with overwhelming support from the "Lincoln" Republican Party (not the Republican Party of the twenty-first century, because this Republican Party has been hijacked by the Southern-Dixiecrat Party and the Tea Party).

There is a political revolution going on in the world community. It is what might be called the political participation explosion. The belief that ordinary individuals are politically relevant and should be involved in the political system has taken firm hold throughout the world. Individuals who have been outside of political systems and without power or influence are demanding their share of political governing power. Question: is the social fabric of American society coming unglued? Obviously, where there is strife, immoral confusion rules because nothing good can come from confusion. On the one hand, the Supreme Court curtails the ability of America to hold fair and just elections; on the other hand, it philosophically embraces same-sex marriage rights when no individual can be born through same-sex relationships. Where are we headed? I hope not to hell in a handbasket. All men and women of goodwill should come together as one nation under God with liberty and justice for all. This means you.

19 TRAYVON MARTIN: THE AFTERMATH

We live in an age of spiritual and moral confusion. Skin color is still more important than moral character. When will America overcome its racial divide and live up to its universal creed, "We hold these truths to be self-evident that all men are created equal...."? The twenty-first century is characterized by guided missiles and mostly misguided men (not women). Americans are being socialized into living societal life under the power and influence of guns rather than godly morality. In a gun culture, guns become god. Currently there are over 300 million guns in American society. Indeed, God is dead in the moral conscience of many secular-minded non-churchgoing Americans. Of course, the spiritual and moral leadership of many churches leaves a lot to be desired. The fact that too many pastoral leaders are preaching to get along rather than to tell the truth is a serious societal problem.

We can only reiterate and live by the words of Jesus the Righteous One: "Put up again thy sword into his place: for all that take the sword shall perish with the sword. Thinkest thou that I cannot pray to my Father, and he shall presently give me more than twelve legions of angels? But how then shall the scriptures be fulfilled, that thus it must be?" (Matthew 26:52-54).

The notion of "stop and frisk" is not a new law enforcement tactic; it has always been an unwritten and unspoken law, especially in the South. For a moment, let's step back in time and analyze the historical law enforcement precedence in minority communities. Law enforcement in minority communities has always been a constabulary designed to keep minorities in a position of mental and physical servitude to dominant culture, especially blacks because of chattel slavery. It is for this reason alone that we must rid law enforcement of racial profiling.

In the formative years of these United States of America, there were slave states and free states. On the one hand, both chattel slaves as well as indentured servants were the property of white slaveholders and therefore could be dealt with in any manner slaveholders so desired. But, on the other hand, Native Americans chose death (liberty) rather than chattel slavery.

After the Civil War, the slogan "go west, young man" became the battlecry for Western frontier expansionism. Of course, in the process Native Americans were almost annihilated because of the gun. The desire for gold and land created the suicidal destruction called the Wild, Wild West. The Wild, Wild West was immorality at its apex. Therefore, greed created a law-and-order organizational constabulary in order to protect the greedy. "Shoot first and ask questions later" became the order of the day, to protect ill-gotten gains.

Southern states and borderline states created a first line of defense to protect the property rights of whites—that is, a "law-and-order" defense system called police departments. This was done to legally intimidate and murder minorities and keep them living in constant fear of physical death, all done in the name of law and order. Of course, this state of affairs has not changed very much, even in the twenty-first century.

Trayvon Martin died because of an immoral bigoted act and an even more nonsensical law: the "stand-your-ground" law.[10] To be sure, professional police officers in many instances utilize this same approach, and even though they may have had psychological and cultural sensitivity training, oftentimes they end up with the same results: an unwarranted death of an American citizen.

Trayvon Martin was profiled and hunted down as if he were a legally convicted common criminal and had no civil rights but to die. Of course, the senseless taking of life is an unacceptable reality regardless of skin tone.

In the conclusion of the matter, it can be profoundly said: "For verily I say unto you, till heaven and earth pass, one jot or one tittle shall in no wise pass from the law, till all be fulfilled. Whosoever therefore shall break one of these least commandments, and shall teach men so, he shall be called the least in the kingdom of heaven…" (Matthew 5:18-19). These things are being revealed daily, and God's judgment in the last days is soon to be fulfilled.

---

10   On February 26, 2012, seventeen-year-old Trayvon Martin was shot and killed by twenty-eight-year-old George Zimmerman in Sanford, Florida. Zimmerman claimed that he shot Martin (who was unarmed) in self-defense and was later acquitted of second-degree murder and manslaughter charges. (Source: Wikipedia.)

20 "STAND YOUR GROUND" IS UNHOLY GROUND

"Stand-your-ground" law is not holy ground; it is a spiritual sickness that places individuals under the power and influence of guns rather than the power and influence of God and godly morality. Under these ungodly laws, many individuals will inherit nothing more than three feet by six feet of ground. When Moses came face-to-face with the reality of God in the form of a non-consuming burning bush, God told Moses to take off his shoes in the presence of holiness, because the ground was holy ground, signifying the sacredness of life and the power of God over life. Furthermore, Moses was told to touch the rock, and out of anger he struck the rock in violation of the will of God. Disobedience, violence, and Moses's state of mind kept him from entering the Promised Land. "How shall we escape, if we neglect so great salvation; which at first began to be spoken by the Lord" (Hebrews

2:3). God has told us in the Ten Commandments given to Moses on Mt. Sinai that "Thou shall not kill." Life is sacred, and if an individual cannot create life from the dust of the ground (nothingness), then an individual should not take life from what God has created.

Stand-your-ground laws are Caesar's way of putting individuals in the ground. All of us should bring to mind what happened to Caesar. Again, the Bible says, "Thou shalt not kill." God made a man from the dust of the ground and did not give any man a license to put another man in the ground. Stand your ground is a license to murder in the name of law and order, and at the same time render your salvation to the devil.

Universal law is about moral conscience and godly morality. Stand-your-ground laws are particularistic and have the potential to give a certain category of individuals the societal right, privilege, and even license to kill under the guise of law and order. (Case in point: Trayvon Martin.) Stand-your-ground laws are unholy because the guilty can easily become the innocent, and the innocent can become the guilty simply because they are alive.

A pistol-packing, bigoted, prejudicial man has no reason to scream for help. Of course, a child walking with a bag of Skittles and a soda pop has every reason to scream in fear when confronted with the reality of a life-and-death situational conflict, especially when the child does not have a gun. Without a doubt, stand-your-ground laws are the devil's playground and potentially America's killing ground. The devil's playground becomes his holy ground to kill the innocent. In fact, stand-your-ground laws can potentially become the basis for societal annihilation. Violence begets violence. Americans should give moral peace a chance.

Historically, minorities have had problems receiving equal justice under the law from professional policing agencies and departments, even though professional policemen are trained in the niceties of cultural sensitivities. Why then would society want to institute laws that give individual citizens the authority to become their own private policing agencies? This is devilish insanity to the *nth* degree. When a private citizen disobeys a direct order from the police department and becomes his own police department, judge, jury, and executioner, we are headed for eternal damnation. "Verily, verily I say unto you, He that heareth my word, and believeth on him that sent me, hath everlasting life, and shall not come into condemnation, but is passed from death unto life" (John 5:24).

God despises prejudice and racism. Aaron and Miriam's anger at Moses's marriage to the Cushite woman caused God to descend from heaven in a pillar of cloud and stand at the doorway of the tent. Scripture says the anger of the Lord burned against them (Numbers 12:1-16).

God forbid if minority mothers tell their sons to "strap it on" in order to stand their ground, because given minority hand-eye coordination, we will have hell on earth rather than heaven on earth. Without a doubt, no mother wants to bury a child; it is not the natural order of things. The glorification of the Wild, Wild West only exists in the movies; it is not holy ground. Proving who is the fastest has a foregone conclusion. As Americans, we must learn to live beyond the graveyard mentality of the Old West.

I am not an angry black man but a God-fearing man, because the fear of God is wisdom. "The fear of the Lord is the beginning of wisdom, and the knowledge of the Holy One is understanding" (Proverbs 9:10). Therefore, above all "do not fear those who can kill the body, but are unable to kill the soul; but rather fear Him who is able to destroy both soul and body in hell" (Matthew 10:28). So be it!

21 AN ANALYSIS OF THE POLITICAL PARTY SYSTEM IN AMERICA

Politics in American society has devolved into an ungodly partisan political power struggle, rather than universal governance oriented toward maximizing the common good. This unfortunate set of circumstances is due to the super-rich and the rich instituting a zero-sum economic game: the super-rich win and the American people lose. What is fueling this socio-political-economic approach is the fact that one political party is married to this super-rich philosophical approach and the other political party is engaged to be married. In the final analysis, the "Corporate Party" wins and the American people lose.

In American society, roughly 2 percent of the population received over 70 percent of the nation's increase in wealth since the economic recovery of 2008. Economically, over 50 percent of the American population cannot come up with two thousand dollars in thirty days.

Women only earn seventy-seven cents for every dollar men earn, and, at the same time, in the majority of households in America, women are the primary wage earners. These facts suggest that many white voters, especially white males, vote against their own best economic interests. The question is, why?

Both political parties are committing societal adultery; greed is greed, and there are no degrees of greed. This set of political circumstances has created a dysfunctional system for our major political parties: the Republican Party and Democratic Party. Currently, both major political parties have their moral and political shortcomings. And of course the "spiritual" principles of social democracy suffer because of political-governance confusion. Both major political parties to varying degrees are guilty of dividing America in the worst kind of way: dividing families and dividing the rich from the poor. It has been said: "If you did it unto the least of them, you did it unto me."

Initially the Republican Party was based upon sound doctrinal governing principles and a commonsense "big-tent" approach to governance. As time passed, because of the Civil Rights Act of 1964 and the Voting Rights Act of 1965, the Republican Party began to embrace the "Southern Dixiecrat" political philosophy concerning power, economic advantage, and political electability. And of course the seedbed for this political approach was Goldwater's limited government strategy, which culminated in Reaganomics. Couple the John Birch Society with Reaganomics, and this philosophy made many rural and suburban dwellers feel as though minorities were getting "something for nothing." This is the case because the Republican Party has become primarily a Southern regional party.

Sad as it is, the Republican Party is functioning upon a political model that is obsolete. Additionally, President Reagan coined politically emotional phrases to galvanize independent voters and rural and suburban dwellers, such as "welfare queen," "giveaway social programs," and "law and order." The current two-party political system has polarized American society and created social-class prejudice rather than societal spiritual unity. In fact, major political parties have so polarized politics and governance in American society that many Americans now define themselves as Independents—that is, in the middle of nothingness.

Also sadly, too many politicians are concerned with the next election rather than the next generation. Instead of planning to plant trees, they are cutting down trees. Unlike the Republican Party, the Democratic Party has a "big-tent" progressive political philosophy and therefore can absorb more readily different kinds of political philosophies and factions. To be sure, sometimes this philosophical political approach creates unbridled factionalism as well.

The Tea Party is an "ultra-cultural," conservative, exclusionary faction of the Republican Party. Seemingly, its primary objective is to hang on the front door of the Republican Party a subliminal message: whites only; no minorities wanted. These types of signs actually existed prior to the 1964 Civil Rights Act and the Voting Rights Act of 1965. Living in the past is not a healthy political strategy, nor is this approach a sound strategy for societal spiritual unity. The past was not perfect; it belongs to the devil, and the future belongs to God. The present moment belongs to individuals. The Tea Party also appears to be "anti-fairness" and more interested in acquiring economic privileges than in equitable inclusion in political governance.

At the same time, the Republican Party has positioned itself as anti-minority, and the voting numbers tend to bear out this socio-political analysis. Every individual votes in his or her own best self-interest and therefore identifies with the political party that advocates their best interests. It appears as though Democratic Party policies are in the best interests of minorities, the nation, and the international community. In the past, Republican Party policies were in the best interests of minorities, the nation, and the international community.

Seemingly, our European allies are more in agreement with America's current "diplomatic" approach to international problem solving than the Republican Party's, whose approach to resolving international issues appears to be militarism. America should never give comfort to or aid her foes, foreign or domestic.

The Minority Party, because of the hijacking of the Republican Party by the Tea Party, has been politically forced into almost wholly aligning itself with the Democratic Party. This in and of itself is spiritually, politically, and economically unhealthy for the well-being of the nation. The Minority Party must always be inclusive. Jesus was about inclusion because all have sinned and come short of the glory of God.

All political parties should be inclusive—that is, they should be of the people, by the people, and for the people. Without a doubt, power for the sake of power is intellectual insanity. In order to have societal unity and world peace, there must be godly spiritual purposes associated with the exercise of power. "The earth is the Lord's and the fullness thereof" (Psalm 24:1), and "it is appointed unto men once to die, but after this the judgment" (Hebrews 9:27).

Godly men and women understand this universal power principle. Therefore, when individuals are faithful over a few things, they will know how to rule (exercise power) over many things. God has spoken to every generation, and His message (theology) from one generation to the next has not changed. Even in the twenty-first century, God is still changing deserts into green pastures (and vice versa). Therefore, all that we say and do should glorify God and be designed to love and serve each other in the spirit of unity of national purpose and above all world peace.

22

A PHILOSOPHICAL ANALYSIS OF REPUBLICANISM

Why are Americans talking about change and at the same time things remain the same? Or why do things change and still seem to remain the same? Of course, we know that "there is an appointed time for everything. And there is a time for every event under heaven" (Ecclesiastes 3:1-10). The greatest change of all comes at death. No matter how good or evil you are or have been the great social equalizer is death. "It is appointed unto men once to die, but after this the judgment" (Hebrews 9:27). Of course, the eternal change is soul salvation and being born again spiritually. For, after all, this change determines where an individual's soul ends up spiritually.

Jesus declared that unless you are born again, you cannot see the kingdom of God (John 3:3). "Verily, verily I say unto thee, except a man be born of water and of the Spirit, he cannot enter into the Kingdom of

God" (John 3:5). Additionally, Jesus said, "Marvel not that I said unto thee, ye must be born again" (John 3:7). To be sure, your soul will end up either in heaven or hell. The choice is an individual one to be made while you are yet physically alive. "But these are written, that ye might believe that Jesus is the Christ, the Son of God, and that believing ye might have life through his name" (John 20:31). Anything less than total commitment is playing judgment games with the adversary, the devil. "And this is life eternal, that they might know thee the only true God, and Jesus Christ, whom thou hast sent" (John 17:3).

This is what God demands of all of us: "Be sober, be vigilant; because your adversary the devil, as a roaring lion, walketh about, seeking whom he may devour: whom resist steadfast in the faith" (1 Peter 5:8-9a). Of course, there is a flipside to these profound biblical truths. "But he that believeth not shall be damned" (Mark 16:16). Finally, God is "angry with the wicked every day" (Psalm 7:11); for historical biblical references, see the stories of Adam and Eve, Noah and the Ark, Abraham and Lot, and Sodom and Gomorrah. "Nevertheless the foundation of God standeth sure, having this seal, The Lord knoweth them that are his" (2 Timothy 2:19).

The reason why things remain the same is because some human beings desire to play god—that is, to be in charge without understanding that all of us are children of God. The desire to be in charge has become greater than the desire to do justly, love mercy, and to walk humbly with God (Micah 6:8). But playing God is a dangerous proposition.

So where does Republicanism go from here? Some say Republicanism needs to go straight to hell. Others say to the glory of God. Former Senator Robert Dole recently declared that Republicanism needs to go under reconstruction. Apparently, the camp that an individual embraces depends on regionalism and biblical perspective. If Republicanism were biblically based rather than dominant-culture based, embraced the common universal good, and exemplified decency and good order, then it would be blessed by heaven. But unfortunately twenty-first-century Republicanism is too particularistic and culturally exclusionary. It excludes rather than creatively includes.

The overwhelming majority of blacks and other ethnic minorities are biblical conservatives but not secular conservatives (which pits human being against human being). Twenty-first-century Republicanism is boldly asking blacks and other ethnic minorities to be against themselves and their own self-interests in order to be Republicans, or to make self the enemy. "No way, Jose." Most blacks, as well as other ethnic minorities, know the way to San Jose. Suicide is indeed insanity.

Republicanism must rethink its regionalism perspective about how politics are done, alter its value orientation, and restructure its approach to coalition building. But most of all, Republicans who are fiscal conservatives and grounded in fair play must reserve the right to vehemently disagree with certain so-called conservative radio-talk show hosts, as well as certain Fox News analysts. This must be done in order that Republicanism might regain the moral high ground and a vision that includes all Americans. Many individuals (and the devil) have used Scripture for evil purposes (for example, during the Civil War). Scriptures are quoted in this essay as an expression of obedience to God's sovereign will, not as an instrument of destruction aimed at the Republican Party.

America needs a viable two-party political system oriented toward the best interests of all and which promotes moral civility between adversaries. Of course, all things are not morally upright in the Democratic Party; there is plenty of room for moral instruction and character improvement.

23   A SOCIO-THEOLOGICAL ANALYSIS OF VANITY

Why are so many Americans in an uproar and so many more Americans devising vain things? To a large degree, the answer lies in the feminizing of American culture, the mass media entertainment industry, and the lustful greed for money. When you get right down to it, instant gratification is at the crux of the problem. The wisest man who has ever lived said it best: "All is vanity" (Ecclesiastes 3:19b). Chasing after pleasure is dangerous to your spiritual well-being. God gives every individual a spiritual test, and the test results are in: "There is no advantage of men over beasts. They have the same breath and both die." "Professing themselves to be wise, they became fools" (Romans 1:22). When you think you know more than God, you are indeed a fool. The real question is, "Where were you when the foundations of the earth were formed?"

"Fools make a mock at sin: but among the righteous there is favor" (Proverbs 14:9). Sin is not a civil rights issue. Sin is a spiritual and moral issue. But some men who think themselves to be wise but are foolish in the sight of God have made sin a governmental civil rights issue. But God does not make mistakes. There is a time and place for all things under the sun. In short, there is a right time and a right place for everything. But some even say that there is a right way to do wrong. "For all have sinned, and come short of the glory of God" (Romans 3:23). From this declaration, let me take you to a higher level of transfiguration: "Therefore, being justified by faith, we have peace with God through our Lord Jesus Christ: by whom also we have access by faith into this grace wherein we stand, and rejoice in hope of the glory of God" (Romans 5:1-2). Knowing the difference and seizing the moment is the key. In short, an individual cannot sleepwalk through life.

A visionary leadership mentality forms the foundation of every strong society. George Washington had such a mentality. Abraham Lincoln had such a mentality. Franklin D. Roosevelt had such a mentality. Therefore, when the leadership foundation is corrupted, society perishes. "Except the Lord of hosts had left unto us a very small remnant, we would have been as Sodom and we would have been like unto Gomorrah" (Isaiah 1:9). God left a remnant of a "few good men" to guide and direct us through trying and perilous times.

It is definitely not the Republicans, because they have become too negative. And of course it is not the Democrats, because they have become too progressive. God is not a God of conservative cultural negativity, and He is definitely not a God of progressive feminized vanity. "For those who guide this people are leading them astray; and those who are guided by them are brought to confusion" (Isaiah 9:16). For it is written, "Whosoever believes that Jesus is the Christ is born of God, and whoever loves the Father loves the child born of Him" (1 John 5:1). For after all, God is life.

The breakdown of family life (into single-parent households), and the moral failure of the Christian church and its unbridled monetary orientation for materialism (church buildings) rather than spirituality (community development), is what is fueling the flames of immoral fleshly vanity. Couple cultural Christianity with stand-your-ground laws born out of ethnic fear (which invariably makes cowards of us all), and what we have is mass societal confusion. The principle of unwarranted fear is what is motivating such laws. Enforcement of such laws is always the problem, not necessarily the laws themselves.

The feminizing of America is born out of an over materialistic, vanity-centered perspective on life, simply because it has become easier for some men to become passive rather than stand up like God-fearing men. This passivity, or feminization, does not necessarily mean homosexuality. This phenomenon exists because too many illegitimate parents are placing their pleasure-principle vanity needs above their parental responsibility and the developmental needs of their children. Of course, what is operating behind the matriarchal society scene in which we live is that it is easier for females, especially minority females, to become meaningfully/gainfully employed. This is a central contributing factor to the feminization of America, and of course this economic set of circumstances is fueling spiritual and social conflict between men and women.

As the sole providers of their families' basic material/survival needs, too many single mothers are teaching their male children to love their mothers and hate their fathers. Children are very impressionable, and they learn through imitation. Therefore, adults should be careful of the examples they set. Female children are taught by their mothers "Don't depend on a man: get an education," and of course male children get caught up in the same social vortex. This is not the full picture of the feminizing of American culture, only a snapshot view. The operative expression used by many women is "I can do bad all by myself."

Too much enmity exists between men and women, and institutional Christianity is not helping to foster the spiritual and moral principle that America was founded on, which is "in God we trust." If men and women do not trust God and the Word of God, there is no way that they can trust each other. Without a doubt, the prison system is designed to feminize men. And who is in prison?

Society begins and ends in the family, and when family structure disintegrates, society becomes spiritually and morally bankrupt because there is no spiritual/moral structure informing what we think, say, or do. To alleviate the negative consequences of an instant gratification, vanity-oriented American society, the family structure, the church, and educational institutions must be spiritually and morally revamped. One "side" does not fit all. Centralized bureaucratic madness is not working. We need to change the centralized madness in our educational systems to holistic community-oriented education—that is, the holistic educational development of family, church, and school. This is the only way we can overcome the devastating conditions of social vanity that are eroding away the spiritual foundation of American society. The overriding issue is moral and spiritual integration, not ethnic/racial integration, because no society can exist unless individuals have a moral conscience. When individuals have moral peace with God, they have societal peace with each other. So be it.

24 AN ANALYSIS OF HOMOSEXUALITY: SOCIAL ISOLATIONISM

Homosexuality poses some perplexing questions. Why does it exist? What are its social and moral implications? How can it be eliminated?

Homosexuality is a direct result of the institutional structure of American society, which encourages and indeed rewards lies, sexism, racism, economic exploitation, and above all homosexuality. Institutional structures dictate the form and shape of human relationships. A lie creates a communication block (social isolationism) because a lie is a mental delusion.

Thus the extraordinary rise and societal public exposure of homosexuality is the clearest indicator that the social system is symbolically intercoursing with itself (self-destructing). The astounding ubiquity of homosexuality is a warning signal that American society is in need of an "enema" (i.e., a value overhaul). Sex is the gut and creative impulse of a community and civilized society. When sexuality is denigrated ("thingified" and commercialized solely for pleasure), environmental quality of life declines and society begins to decay morally. Life is not a freebie, and least of all is sexuality. The story of Adam and Eve in the Garden of Eden teaches this profound lesson.

Why then the phenomenal rise and societal exposure of homosexuality? Could it be that capitalism as an economic system is so materialistic and dehumanizing that it engenders social isolationism rather than social integration? Consequently, individuals seek to maximize the pleasure principle: pleasure without pain is the name of the game. Strange politics usually leads to strange bedfellows. When men and women do not share the same political views about life, it is difficult for them to share the bedroom. Homosexuality is highly correlated with the oldest lie in the human community, sexism. Indeed, the Women's Liberation Movement is seemingly a response to arbitrary and artificial role definitions (exploitation).

As previously discussed, the economic structure of American society dictates the form and nature of all other social processes. Job opportunities determine lifestyles. Finding and maintaining gainful employment is a symbol of personhood. At the same time, the world of work is dominated by such parochial notions as privilege, racism, sexism, and so on. Therefore, the institutional structure of society defines social roles. When an economic structure excludes numerous individuals and defines them as parasites, then social role models become blurred. Work then is mankind's basic form of self-actualization, and when it is dehumanized society creates a Pandora's Box. Thus, economic processes that are solely designed to exploit special units in a society (women and ethnic minorities) create isolationism, alienation, powerlessness, self-estrangement, normlessness, and above all self-withdrawal. Economic exploitation encourages lie accommodation (unrighteousness), and homosexuality is a lie. God created one door, not a back door. Back doors are usually lies. Homosexuality is a back door. Blacks are very familiar with the dehumanizing effects of having to use back doors.

What are the effects of economic exploitation on the family structure? Family is the significant socializer because society begins with the family. Hence, family is universally viewed as the basis for societies. Environmental socialization is the key to differences in human behavior. Thus, family socialization shapes the standards of male and female roles. Capitalism as an economic system is so repressive that it militates against family life—e.g., divorce rates, separation, desertion, and so on. All of these forms of family and societal disorganization are usually caused by economic pressures.

Therefore, mental temperament is not defined by sex (biology) but by family socialization and environmental socialization into a culture (economic responsibility). A male child learns how to become a male and father by observing a father role model. Likewise, a female child learns how to become a woman and mother by observing a mother role model. When these role models are blurred and distorted because of human exploitation and social isolationism, life becomes a ball of confusion. Personality structures can be altered by changing processes of socialization, because values dictate the form and shape of social processes and institutional structures. Therefore, drug usage and homosexuality are "destructive" quests for personal and societal meaning. That is, when individuals ask what the purpose of life and existence is, these questions are essentially questions about meaning and being (ontology), and therefore are religious questions. That is, the problem of meaning is essentially a religious question.

Individualism and human exploitation create chaos, not community. Unrighteousness creates despair, but righteousness creates hope. America needs a national symbol of hope and collective integrity. The church can provide such a symbol, but it too is in dire need of an enema (a spiritual value reorientation). Church should be about spirituality and communalism, not materialism. Church should be about character building (spiritual/intellectual integrity), not material empire building. Unfortunately, the church is the most successful form of vulgar capitalism and rugged individualism in the modern world. The Christian church, because of its value orientation, can absorb all of the exploitative processes of secular society, at the same time minimize the negative consequences, and in so doing not pay taxes. Institutional religion has identified itself wholly with secular culture and therefore has lost its prophetic power to speak the truth in *love*.

Humankind was created by truth and love, and not to be naturally good is to lie to self. Hence, homosexuality is a lie and simply another way for modern humankind to be sinful and unrighteous, because the structure of society makes it difficult for one to exercise righteousness (moral integrity). In American society, to love truth is tantamount to self-denial because to be truthful will probably cost one his job and possibly his life. Homosexuality simply says that mankind cannot handle freewill choice. Animals are programmed to mate only when they can procreate their species' kind. Mankind is the most intelligent being in creation and at the same time the most confused. Humans can participate in sexuality for pleasure. In our attempt to maximize the pleasure principle, we invariably distort nature, attempting to make God/nature a liar.

Therefore, if the human mind and soul are confused, whatever ideas are generated by the mind invariably will cause confusion and chaos. The ubiquity of homosexuality should not surprise anyone, since nearly everything we do we decide to do unrighteously rather than righteously. When one loses his or her mind, invariably soul is also lost. Finally, a great society knows when the ship has sprung an irreparable leak, and the captain summons the ship ashore. But, more importantly, the greatness of a people is measured by the strength of their collective character and not the ship they built.

Life is about the development of character traits: competence, integrity, understanding, knowledge, and above all self-discipline. Heterosexual love is based on materialism rather than responsibility. Homosexual love is based upon vanity-seeking pleasure, which is exploitation without materialism or intellectualism. Therefore, homosexuality expresses the compartmentalization of love. To be sure then, homosexuality is the apex of self-estrangement.

Blessed, O Lord, is the society that seeks not to compartmentalize love, social-cost accountability, and above all collective social responsibility.

25   SAME-SEX MARRIAGE: CIVIL RIGHT OR HUMAN RIGHT?

O ver the past two decades there have been calculated efforts toward identifying the Gay Rights Movement with the Civil Rights Movement of the 1960s. The Constitution declares that "we hold these truths to be self-evident that all men are created equal and endowed with certain inalienable rights from their Creator." Therefore, America has always clearly differentiated between civil rights and human rights. Human rights are God-given rights. Civil rights are granted by society, and of course this is why blacks were denied their civil rights even though they were American citizens. If an individual is born in America, citizenship is an automatic given. The practice of homosexuality is a human right because it is grounded in the concept of free will, and therefore it cannot be viewed as an issue of civil rights. Homosexuality is private behavior between consenting adults; it is a sexual behavior that takes place behind closed doors and should remain behind closed doors.

Marriage is for children, not adults. This is precisely why children born out of wedlock are called illegitimate, when in fact the parents are the ones who are illegitimate, because they were together for vanity and pleasure seeking and not out of godly love for each other. The child is conceived and, if brought to term, gets here the same way as everyone does. To God then sexuality and marriage are one and the same. Sexuality is God's freewill gift to humans, because we have a personal choice in the matter—that is, we can participate in sexuality both for pleasure as well as procreation. Therefore, to God, any form of human sexuality outside of marriage is sin (fornication, adultery, and homosexuality). Of course, from God's viewpoint, the purpose of sexuality can be found in the fourfold foundation of Genesis 1:27-28: "be fruitful, multiply, replenish, and subdue." Lower forms of animal life are biologically programmed to participate in sexual acts only for procreation purposes, not pleasure. Sexuality as a way for human beings to give each other pleasure is a gift from God and should not become a curse.

Same-sex marriage provides a way for the social system not to have to support fatherless children by allowing same-sex couples to adopt these children. This sinister social policy is based upon propagandist research that says that children who are reared in same-sex families are no more likely to become homosexual than children who are reared in heterosexual families. Same-sex couples cannot procreate homosexuality; they must recruit.

God (the Creator) cannot violate His own principles. Again, homosexuality is a personal sexual preference (a pleasure-principle choice) that is grounded in an expression of free will. God is not a divine dictator of human choices. Nor is God a divine Santa Claus, whom you can ask what you will and it is granted. This confusion has led to the popularization of homosexuality in our culture among young people.

Thus, as a culture, rather than talking about societal responsibilities, we are talking about societal rights (such as gay rights and same-sex marriage rights). The goal of society is self-perpetuation, not self-annihilation. Because no individual is called into being (born into this world) through homosexuality or same-sex marriage, they are counter forces to societal perpetuation. We all get here the same way—the front door, not the back door.

Philosophically, same-sex relations are the ultimate form of self-denial and self-rejection. Sex is a status category, and the categories are male and female. Sex status is biological, not sociological. Human sexuality (gender identity) can be expressed heterosexually or homosexually, which in turn becomes preferential participatory choice. Therefore, homosexuality is not grounded in biology, because biologically the sexual feelings of a man are outward and the sexual feelings of a woman are inward. After all, to reject the biology of your own physical anatomy is likewise to reject the divinity of your being (soul). This is why the Bible declares that God gives homosexuality over to a reprobate mind. It is in the mind, not the behind.

Simply put, homosexuality is the ultimate expression of self-centeredness (egoism)—that is, an individual who has turned inward to serve his own egotistical vanity needs. Ego then becomes an acronym for Edge God Out. Finally, God's command is that human beings be fruitful (produce God-fearing children), multiply, and replenish the earth, not participate in self-annihilation.

To be sure, marriage as a social institution is based in gender statuses (male/female) and most of all the reproduction of those statuses. The most important statuses in society are father/mother, grandfather/grandmother, son/daughter, and so on. Homosexuality, like heterosexuality, is about human sexual activity. But homosexuality is simply sexual activity, not based in gender status. Without a doubt, homosexual sex cannot reproduce the statuses of male/female, and of course homosexual sex cannot reproduce a status called homosexuality. There are approximately eight billion individuals on the planet, and no individual has his or her origin grounded in homosexuality. Gender identity (status) is determined at the moment of conception, the joining of egg and sperm (when a human being becomes a divine spirit/soul), unseen by the human eye.

Human sexuality is a private act that only concerns consenting adults. Therefore homosexuality is not a civil right but a human right (based upon the concept of free will), where one is free to participate in homosexual acts in the privacy of one's home, hotel, motel, etc. Human sexuality does not require a third-party process, whether politics, public policy, or public opinion. The old adage of "who knows what goes on behind closed doors" is more than applicable in relationship to homosexuality, as well as heterosexuality.

What then is the purpose of society positioning homosexuality (a private sexual act between consenting adults) as an issue of civil rights? If homosexuality is viewed as a civil rights issue, then Pandora's Box is opened as wide as the gates of hell and will result in societal annihilation. To be sure, every known society that has embraced homosexuality has met with inevitable destruction.

For example, we know that there are individuals who engage in sexual acts with animals. Should society sanction marriage between humans and animals, based upon the notion of individual civil rights and property rights? Moreover, does an individual have the civil right to have more than one wife? That is, based upon the notion that I have a civil right to marry my dog, sheep, baboon, and so on, I might bequeath my earthly possessions to my animal sex partner.

The notion of same-sex marriage is an insane slippery slope that society should avoid at all costs. Homosexuality is more about vanity pleasure and ego (men and women turning inward) than the perpetuation of the human species and human society. "For the wrath of God is revealed from heaven against all ungodliness and unrighteousness of men, who hold the truth in unrighteousness; because that which may be known of God is manifest in them; for God has shewed it unto them. For the invisible things of him from the creation of the world are clearly seen, being understood by the things that are made, even his eternal power and Godhead; so that they are without excuse: because that, when they knew God, they glorified him not as God, neither were thankful; but became vain in their imaginations, and their foolish hearts were darkened" (Romans 1:18-23).

Adam and Eve knew what they had done and what the "private" body parts were for, and of course this is why they covered their private (sexual) parts with fig leaves. The proper function of an individual is to live creatively, not merely exist for the sake of the pleasure principle. The moral integration of flesh and spirit is a matter of human will, human conscience, and human morality; only humans can understand morality because only humans are conscious of the meaning of death in relationship to life. The real question is: what is the higher purpose of homosexuality? To be sure, the higher purpose of marriage is the procreation and the protective nurturing of children. Indeed, marriage is for children, not adults, because marriage is about procreation. Life in its fullest, higher dimension is about self-sacrifice and self-discipline, not turning inward to serve one's own ego interests. After all, there are no winners in the non-issue of same-sex marriage. (Someone told me to deliver this message!)

In summation, there is a distinct difference between the concept of civil rights and human rights. Civil rights are rights that societies grant to their citizens. Human rights are universal rights that come from God and have nothing whatsoever to do with societal tenets, structures, processes, and legalities. Therefore, human sexuality is grounded in the concept of freewill choice (a human right) simply because sexuality is a private act, not open to public opinion (politics). What goes on behind closed doors should remain behind closed doors.

For this reason, minority groups in American society being denied certain civil rights based upon skin tone or national origin is vastly different from the gay rights issue. Ethnic/racial identity is far more obvious than a private act. We do not know who is gay unless the individual makes an open declaration or confession. What then is the purpose of an individual participating in a private act behind closed doors and then asking for societal acceptance after the fact? If it matters, why not ask before the fact? I might add that I am not for anyone being denied a job, housing, and access to valued societal resources because they openly declare themselves to be homosexual. I am against institutionalized discrimination of any form or kind.

26 THE ISSUE OF SIN IS DESTROYING THE FABRIC OF AMERICAN SOCIETY

"**W**herefore, as by one man sin entered into the world, and death by sin; and so death passed upon all men, for all have sinned" (Romans 5:12). In all of these spiritual teachings, I acknowledge that I render unto Caesar that which belongs to Caesar, and I render unto God that which belongs to God, because all good and perfect gifts come from God. Legalizing and commercializing sin is not an effective godly strategy for dealing with sin, especially for a society whose Constitution is biblically/spiritually grounded. Nor can you solve the problem of sin with guns and bombs. Only love and the practice of love overcome sin.

The problem of sin comes from a moral separation from God, both individual and societal. A saint is a sinner saved by God's grace and mercy through the birth, teachings, death, resurrection, and ascension of Jesus

Christ. "For whatsoever is born of God overcometh the world, even our faith. Who is he that overcometh the world, but he that believeth that Jesus is the Son of God?" (1 John 5:4-5). Based upon the rampant nature of sin that now characterizes American culture, America is truly in need of a rebirth of the human spirit. "For he hath made him to be sin for us, who knew no sin; that we might be made the righteousness of God in him" (2 Corinthians 5:21).

Again, sin is moral separation from the reality of God as ultimate truth. All human beings sin and fall short of the glory and expectations of God. There is no such animal as a little sin or big sin. Sin is sin. However, if individuals commit the same sin over and over again, then God gives them over to a reprobate mind (Romans 1:28-32).

In analyzing the term "human being," we can readily discern that the word "human" is a compound word. "Hu" comes from the word "humus," or dirt. As humans, our bodies were made from dirt. "Man" refers to mind. It is in the mind that our souls are housed. God gives each individual a mind with free will—that is, the freedom of choice. No individual can take freewill choice away from another individual. Finally, the concept of "being" is ontological in nature (i.e., spiritual). Yet we are becoming more materialistic rather than more spiritual.

Human sexuality is the most private of all human activities. Sexuality should be closed-door business between consenting adults in the manner in which God ordained. In other words, human sexuality is not a civil right; it is private and personal business. I must vehemently confess: "Lay hands suddenly on no man, neither be partaker of other men's sins: keep thyself pure" (1 Timothy 5:21). Every individual has his/her own personal sin (cross to bear); therefore we should not help another person to sin. Instead, we should always bring to the attention of others that the wages of sin is death, but the gift of God is eternal life through Jesus Christ our Lord and Savior (Romans 6:23). The Holy Bible is the only standard for judging what sin is. God commands that we love one another because He loves us so much that He gave His only begotten Son for our soul salvation (John 3:16). This is why we must always disapprove of sin. "Love the sinner and have hatred for the sin, because sin is of the devil."

Without a doubt, an A is an A, just as a V is a V. They have different sounds phonetically, as well as different functions in the alphabetical system. On the one hand, taking an A, flipping it upside down, and removing the crossbar in no way alters the phonetic sound—that is, its purpose. An A is still an A and a V is still a V. On the other hand, taking the "cross" out of human affairs alters everything. For, after all, the cross is about individual/collective responsibility. God and nature ordained the V body part to be the vehicle for birthing life. The A body part is the vehicle for death excretion. Exchanging body part processes in order to maximize the pleasure principle in no way alters the divine/natural purpose.

A clarion call has been issued. The opportunity has come. The question is, what shall we do with the country that God has tremendously blessed to be the spiritual and moral light of the world? America's internal morality cannot be based upon an "each to his own way" philosophy. When you get right down to it, human self-centeredness fosters spiritual and moral bankruptcy. The big game is over! The federal government does far more good than bad; therefore Americans should insist with godly fervor that the government not legalize sin. Only the devil wants sin legalized. American culture has become too materialistic and paganistic. Indeed, America is on the brink of a spiritual and moral collapse into chaos. When God-fearing Americans see the writing on the wall, we need to declare that enough is enough. God gave Noah the rainbow sign: no more water, but fire the next time. Sodom and Gomorrah serve as a classic example of the judgment of Almighty God. So be it.

27 A SOCIO-RELIGIOUS ANALYSIS OF THE ECOLOGICAL CRISIS: HUMAN EXPLOITATION

The human mind is like unto a parachute;
in order to function at the junction it must be open.

Anonymous Christianity is a powerful idea about collective responsibility, human values, and above all human character development. What contributions can the Christian tradition offer to the resolution of the current ecological crisis?

The ecological crisis depicts two overriding dilemmas: (1) resource depletion and (2) environmental denigration. The cause of resource waste is not commonly recognized as a problem of human values. Making the environmental crisis invisible is easier than curing the cause.

That is, it is easier to deal with symptoms of the environmental crisis rather than deal with the root cause (negative values and human exploitation). Therefore, technology, production, delivery systems, and the utilization and disposal of resources are not the causes of resource waste but are symptomatic of the larger problems of human values, human exploitation, and the failure of mankind to integrate ideas. Thus the question of "environmental quality" and the causes of the environmental crisis cannot be evaded forever. Will we be exploiters of creation or Godlike caretakers of creation?

The environmental crisis also raises serious questions about individual and societal meaning: How do we live? What are we willing to give up? How do we transform collective interest into collective action? How do we learn to resolve conflict nonviolently?

Current resolutions to the environmental crisis are individualistic and oriented toward special interest groups and therefore do not address the basic problems of axiology (mindset), institutional structures, human values, and social structures that are designed for exploitation. Appropriate or alternate technology is not the solution to the current environmental crisis. A reshaping of humankind's value orientation is needed. That is, humankind must value the whole creation, rather than only valuing personal redemption and personal salvation, or individual survival. The ecological crisis is essentially a crisis of appropriate values rather than technology, because values dictate technological forms, not vice versa.

The ecological crisis depicts a serious cultural lag. By cultural lag, I mean that our material culture is exceeding and leading our spiritual and moral development. Mankind, being obsessed with individual redemption in relationship to creation, has developed sophisticated social structures, social processes, and numerous "creature comforts" (electric toothbrushes, shoe brushes, hairbrushes, knives, forks, and so on). Humankind has left undeveloped the one institution that was given to us by God, which is the church. It was given for humankind's spiritual self-development and moral character development. In other words, there is nothing on the "inside" of man directing what he creates on the "outside" (environment).

Life is about happiness, but happiness is born of internal peace and then moves to the outside. Therefore, the ecological crisis is caused by the failure of human beings to develop both mentally and spiritually. Humankind's spiritual impoverishment causes him to love lies more than the truth and love evil more than good. Mankind's mental impoverishment causes the design of ineffective processes to exploit both the environment and each other, because to be efficient and effective is to be good. Mankind's spiritual impoverishment causes him to travel down the road of self-annihilation.

Hence, the ecological crisis is only symptomatic of the larger problem of a value crisis. Human exploitation as a social value has been institutionalized in our political processes, economic processes, educational processes, and social processes as ways and means of restricting access to valued societal resources. Human exploitation is negativism to the *nth* degree.

Human beings operating negatively toward themselves invariably cause themselves to become negative about their natural habitat—i.e., the universe. It is inconsistent for one to talk of human community and human exploitation in the same breath. Inconsistency breeds moral and ethical bankruptcy.

Therefore, the greatest source of pollution is our mindset and the negative ideas that stem from our worldview and value orientation. The following cross-classification table helps to clarify the issue.

	Axiology (Worldview)	Epistemology	Logic
European	Man/Object	Cognition	Either/Or
Asian	Man/Nature	Co-Native Progress	Set Theory
African	Man/Man	Affective	Both/And (Everything Is Everything)

Therefore, "either/or" logic and the negative assumptions that guide our theory construction and undergird our social processes and social structures are based on extremes rather than the "in between." To be sure, life is about the "in between" rather than extremes, because individuals always find God at the center of life.

Western industrial societies are characterized by scientism. Out of the notion that science is the "cureall," a technical culture has emerged, preponderantly committed to a wholly materialistic style of life. Thus scientism has profoundly altered man's natural habitat, the universe. Humankind's scientific orientation marks a change in the way humans grasp the universe and their lives together. More importantly, Western societies are characterized by a worldview that defines power and values as external to individuals. In fact, power is defined as a zero-sum game. Either you have power or you don't have power.

Historically, different cultural groups have occupied certain territorial spheres and developed different ways of thinking and organizing human life. Ways of societal organization reflect what societies think is the purpose and meaning of life. Obviously, life is not about exploitation but human community. The Christianity that Jesus espoused could not have given rise to vulgar capitalism because Christianity is about collective responsibility, not selfish, individualistic hoarding.

Christianity is about collective stewardship. Could it be that the Protestant ethic and the spirit of capitalism are social fabrications? Loving material things in and of themselves, and human exploitation at the same time, invariably creates waste, pollution, violence, and above all a loss of societal meaning and purpose. Humans seeking to recreate through their own powers an "unreal world" have caused environmental chaos. Thus the ecological crisis does not stem from a lack of technological knowledge and skills. Generating the appropriate technology is the least of our problems.

There are two social processes in life: (1) life in life (collective responsibility and human community) and (2) death in life (human exploitation and self-annihilation). Mankind has consistently chosen death in life to build upon rather than life in life to build upon.

Problems of environmental quality—that is, problems of resource waste—stem from dominant cultural values that facilitated the development of America into the most affluent nation state in the modern world. Yet these negative values, which have legitimized negative institutional structures, are at the *crux* of our environmental crisis. At least four negative values have guided America's affluence:

1. Growth: "the more the better"; the notion that materialism brings happiness
2. Consumption: the belief that consumption causes both progress and prosperity, or external values
3. Technology: the more technology the better; the notion that science is a cureall
4. "Plentiful nature" ethic: the notion that nature is a free resource that is endless in scope

Human exploitation (institutionalized negativism) has not facilitated two important processes that are necessary for the development of the community (local, national, and international):

1. The integration of ideas. If individuals cannot integrate ideas, they will never integrate worldviews and cultures.
2. Systems integration, systems analysis, and above all institutional change strategies

Therefore, resolution of the current ecological crisis will require taking responsibility for both self and society, and some basic changes in value orientation and institutional structures.

Unfortunately, alternate forms of technology are simply modernistic forms of pietism rather than collectivism. Thus individualism, at the expense and exclusion of collectivism, depicts the essence of the human predicament. Modern humanity is a slow learner; for more than two thousand years, we have not demonstrated that we have learned very much at all about life and human interdependence. While living in central cities has economic advantages for minorities, environmentally it is extremely hazardous to health and well-being. To be sure, environmental quality of life for urban dwellers has become increasingly problematic.

American society and the world at large are playing environmental death games; therefore, modern technology reflects (and creates) a culture of death. We must stop playing death games and start the war for life. Mankind's sin against itself is our attempt to improve upon God's creation. In so doing, humans always become guilty of prideful sensuality and eventual self-withdrawal in seeking to serve our own ego interests. False pride brings about human tragedy, suffering, and above all death—symbolically and physically. Without a doubt, when individuals become void of "ethical codes of moral conduct" (inner motives), the socio-spiritual consequences of modern technology are disastrous. Finally, it is the negative ideas of human exploitation that have placed us on the wrong side, fighting against God, natural law, and above all ourselves. Indeed, humankind has become the endangered species.

28 TEN THINGS: BRIDGING THE CULTURAL RACIAL DIVIDE

t is indeed unfortunate that one of the main problems in American society is the color line. However, if America is to survive and thrive as a great nation, we must learn to live beyond the color line—that is, beyond the graveyard. The key is to realize that sin is the issue, not skin pigmentation. On the one hand, the black mindset tends to be a response to "white institutional cultural racism." On the other hand, the white mindset is privilege oriented—that is, whites want privilege without collective social responsibility (i.e., universal public service and accountability).

Jesus's desire was to teach and provide an example of how to live free from negativism. After all, life is about learning, and of course there are some things that blacks can learn from whites, and likewise there are some things that whites can learn from blacks. Social behavior is culturally conditioned, not skin-color conditioned. Conversely, there are some things that whites practice that blacks need to shun vehemently, such as hypocrisy and greediness.

Life is about commitment, public service to others, and determining where we place our ultimate trust. But, more importantly, life is a sharing of responsibility, that infinite obligation each person owes another. It has been said that "the world is a stage, and there is an entrance and an exit, and for every exit there is an entrance." Life constantly moves. Life is dynamic in quality, and therefore the human personality should be adaptable, not static. American cultural life has become static and chaotic rather than dynamic, precisely because blacks and whites cannot live beyond the graveyard of institutional cultural racism and attitudinal racism.

In short, American cultural life is too skin-color coordinated. Right and wrong, truth and lies, and good and bad are not housed in a black-and-white dichotomy. There is a spiritual war being waged in American society. This spiritual war is eating at the very soul of the most profound declaration in the history of humankind: "We hold these truths to be self-evident that all men are created equal and endowed with certain inalienable rights from their Creator...." Sadly, this spiritual war has led to discussions about the right to do wrong (self-centeredness) rather than the responsibility to do the right thing(s). Spike Lee was absolutely correct when he declared in his infamous movie *Do the Right Thing*. Unfortunately, there is cultural confusion in American life about what is right and what is wrong. Notions of right and wrong are conditioned by ethnicity, social class, and popularity (hero worship). Too many individuals in our society take right, turn it into wrong, and make it work—and vice versa.

It is hoped that the thoughts expressed in this book will be viewed as a down payment on making human life more human in American society. Making you your best friend is a lifelong journey because "self" is always the enemy. As a nation, we must institute a character development model that allows individuals to learn how to make themselves their own best friend. To live creatively is to know freedom from fear. To have life more abundantly is to learn self-discipline because self-discipline is a spiritual value. Great living or low-life living involves sacrifice. Jesus always urged the wisdom of anticipating the cost. Pay as you enter. Pay as you leave. Or fly now and pay later, but you must pay.

"Show me the path of life that in thy joy I may dwell, for in thy right hand are pleasures for evermore" (Psalm 16:11). Narrow is the gate that leads to citizenship in the kingdom of God. Broad is the way that leads to destruction. As a nation, we need to get on the King's highway, because sin (wrongdoing) leaves sinners (wrongdoers) defenseless and above all makes us our own enemies as a nation. To be sure, I am fully aware that social behavior is not color specific; behavior is more directly influenced by environment and culture (socialization) than by skin pigmentation.

I suggest the following ten things to help bridge the cultural racial divide between blacks and whites in America:

1. HONORING COMMITMENTS

Life is about commitment. In Genesis 3:8-9, God raises the question of commitment with Adam. Where art thou? Where do you live? Whose side are you on? Whom do you love the more? No matter how one frames the question, life is commitment and commitment is life. Life is about making decisions (choices), and of course choices have consequences (positive and negative). It is in our freewill choice that God ordains freedom. Whites understand the importance of keeping the commitments that an individual makes, even when it is not in the best self-interest of the individual who made the commitments.

The life of Jesus was one of commitment to the will of God. Jesus clearly understood that life is not governed by "blind chance." Instead, life is a response to our deepest yearnings and highest aspirations.

Therefore, whites understand that not to keep the commitments we make is moral failure. In other words, how can we say that we are willing to live by "every word [Bible] that comes out of the mouth of God" and we are not willing to live the words that come out of our own mouths (Matthew 4:4)? Herein lies the issue of reputation and social image. Reputation is about moral character. In the final analysis, reputation is the most important thing that an individual can leave in the world. Therefore, all of us should implicitly understand that if we fail those who look to us, who trust us, then we fall short of realizing who we are, especially when we fail our children.

2. PRACTICING TIME MANAGEMENT

The categories of understanding are essentially religious in nature. Time, space, class, and number are all categories of understanding. Time belongs to God, and as human beings we anticipate eighty to ninety years of healthy space between birth and death. Because of human mortality, time is a precious and limited resource. In fact, mortality helps us to understand morality. Therefore, for humans, life is about what we do with the "dash" between birth and death. It is not about where we start the race but where we end up. An individual has no control over the social and environmental circumstances of his or her birth or death. The question is, how do I live? More importantly, what am I willing to sacrifice in order to live the way I say I want to live?

Starting organizational meetings on time and honoring scheduled appointments and financial obligations in a timely fashion is generally a positive character trait. Time management is a function of self-discipline and self-sacrifice. To be sure, time is not an endless resource, but time is your most important resource—and you must utilize it well. Time belongs to God, and understanding this social fact will help an individual understand his or her limitations (strengths and weaknesses). This is why, generally speaking, whites start meetings and events on time. Take care of the business (agenda) and then move on because time is a precious resource, and you do not have any time to waste. Both success and failure leave a documented trail.

Understanding this dynamic life principle about time produces future conversations about solutions to both family issues and organizational/institutional problems. Ecclesiastes 3:1-8 declares "that there is a time for everything, including every event under heaven." Simply put, because as humans we do not know the appointed time for our physical death, a healthy respect for time is tantamount to showing honor to God. Physical death is an appointment that no individual can cancel. We can cancel business appointments, dental/medical appointments, and casual appointments, but not death appointments. Death is the social equalizer because it does not respect personality and social status differences. Death simply says that we are all equal in dignity before God.

3. SEEKING PSYCHIATRIC COUNSELING SERVICES WHEN NEEDED

When whites blow it oftentimes you never know it, because they are willing to seek professional help. In other words, whites are willing to have professionals help them work through identity crises, family crises, and interpersonal relationship issues. The search for understanding is neither easy nor popular. The truth about human life is still simple, even in the most affluent, complex, technological society on the planet. There is a destiny that makes us one. No individual goes his or her own way. All ways are interconnected. What individuals invest in the lives of others invariably comes back into their own.

4. PURSUING HOMEOWNERSHIP

In general, whites tend to understand that homeownership is the foundation of wealth development, especially legacy wealth. When whites purchase a home, it is not essentially about the individual house. It is about the "neighborhood"—that is, the overall quality of life, including the quality of education offered by the school district, the values (priorities) of the neighbors, and personal safety and security issues for their families. The focus is less on dress and more on address.

There are three keys to the development of legacy wealth and family independence. The first key is homeownership. It is the foundation of the American dream. In American society, everyone buys real estate. The question is, who are you buying it for—yourself or someone else? If you are renting (leasing) or purchasing (paying a mortgage note), you are buying real estate. Since you are buying it one way or the other, then it is best to buy it for yourself rather than someone else.

The second key to economic independence is the ability of an individual to acquire a 401(k) or 403(b). In other words, it is best to have your social security in the bank under your name rather than with the federal government. We live in a private enterprise system whereby capital is in the hands of private individuals, not the government. The federal government can do some things and do them well, such as the interstate highway system. However, the government cannot manage and plan your future financial independence better than you can. If individuals think that the federal government can manage their financial future, they have a much more serious problem than money management. In other words, the individual has a self-management problem.

The third key is that we live in a knowledge-based economy. Acquiring a quality education is an important key to obtaining economic independence. Without a doubt, educational choice for one's children is an essential building block for legacy wealth. In a knowledge-based economy, college degrees, certificates of certification, and specialized training credentials are the currency (money). Knowledge then is wealth.

5. UNDERSTANDING THE AMERICAN CORPORATE BUSINESS MODEL

The corporate business model of American culture is an extension of the extended family concept. Business development in the white community is built upon a corporate business model rather than a church building model. When whites came to America, they came with a cultural system of institutional cooperation based upon the notion of white supremacy. Invariably whites cooperate with each other institutionally, even when they do not personally like each other. In short, whites view their personal economic interests and personal survival as intrinsically bound together. Therefore, whites have built an economic system based upon white institutional cooperation.

In short, their institutions morally affirm the essential divine worth of whiteness. Their love of cooperating with each other transcends personality differences and conflicts. Consequently, white institutions and organizations allow whites to care and share among themselves. To be sure, an organizational structure is about commitment, because structure fosters sharing and caring. In this context, the philosophy that guides business development in the white community is "keep your mind on your money and your mouth shut." Whites have a business philosophy that does not allow them to become fixated on limitations but rather take advantage of the opportunities afforded. In other words, whites believe that you "don't wait for opportunity, you create it." Therefore, their view of greatness is not what an individual can get others to do for him or her, but what an individual can do for self and others. Whites know how to win at all costs with a "bad hand"; it is called partnering.

Business development is about making room for yourself, charting your own course of action, and creating your own future. Risk taking is an admirable character trait in white culture. Bill Gates is the ultimate operative example. Without a doubt, success does not come to you; you must go to it, because success requires patience. Only coffee is instant, not success.

6. VALUING A QUALITY EDUCATION

The notion of universal mass education is what has made America a great society. By and large, white parents will sacrifice immeasurably in order for their children to obtain a quality education. This of course is a double-edged sword because it also helps to ensure that the children of other cultural backgrounds will always be working for white children, even though they will be off the scene (dead). Of course, this helps to perpetuate the self-fulfilling prophecy of white supremacy. To a large degree, obtaining a quality education does level the economic playing field. This is why white parents are usually involved in Parent Teacher Organizations, are more likely than not to attend scheduled teacher-parent conferences, and are more likely than not to attend the extracurricular activities that their children are involved in. The value that whites place on getting a quality education is reflected in the growth of predominantly white church-related charter schools and private schools.

Everything an individual needs to know is in a book. Most whites understand this social fact. Therefore, most whites "think" and "read." Thinking and reading engenders documentation (recordkeeping). Whites will put the pencil on you before God gets the news. Again, we live in a knowledge-based economy. Knowledge is wealth because ideas generate money and wealth. The currency in a knowledge-based economy is a degree, and in many instances an advanced degree or specialization.

7. LETTING THE DEAD BURY THE DEAD

When Jesus was recruiting disciples for His soul-saving work along the shores of the Galilee, one of the disciples said to Jesus that he was willing to follow Him, but he must first go and bury his dead father. Jesus replied, "Follow me and let the dead bury the dead" (Matthew 8:22). In general, whites do not try to change things that they do not have any control over. Learning to mind what matters and to never mind what doesn't is one of the keys to successful living.

Understanding this important principle of life helps an individual reduce negative self-talk and most of all articulate positive themes about the meaning of life. This understanding of life facilitates and encourages the burying of dysfunctional interpersonal relationships (family relations/friendships) and situations. It is this type of thinking that allows whites to truly write their own thanksgiving proclamation and then live thoughtfully, creatively, and thankfully every day. In white culture, every person is required to pull his or her own wagon, and when an individual violates public trust, whites immediately distance themselves from that person, even though they understand that public humiliation serves as a reminder that we are dependent upon other people.

The best example of the positive results of the philosophy of "let the dead bury the dead" is the impact that the Civil Rights Movement had on white mentality. Martin Luther King Jr.'s strategy of nonviolence, epitomized in the phrase "I am trying to love somebody," humbled a racist nation before the world community. Whites not only changed, to a large degree, racist laws and the racist structure of American society, but many whites changed their racist attitudes as well. Many whites simply viewed America as a nation of "doors of opportunities"— that is, they transcended their whiteness. In short, in the civil rights struggle of the 1960s, many whites acquired the spiritual will to live beyond their slave ownership heritage in order to free themselves from the shackles of the sins of their ancestors. It is important to learn how to literally and mentally distance ourselves from dysfunctional relatives and friends.

8. IMITATING IDEAL PARENTAL (FATHER/MOTHER) ROLE MODELS

Everyone has a biological father and mother. However, in modern America, with its high divorce rates and number of single-parent families, many children do not have daddies and mommies. The effect of this breakdown of family life is a fatherless society. Even in the midst of this universal breakdown of family structure in American social life, we all should place moral and spiritual priority on the ideal family structure.

9. UNDERSTANDING THE IMPORTANCE OF ORGANIZATIONAL NETWORKING SKILLS

Institution building is a salient characteristic of white culture. In white culture, one monkey does not stop a show. By and large, white institutions are not personality driven, nor do they operate on the basis of one-person rule. In order for institutions to be effective, they must operate on the principles of structure, function, planning, and coordination. To be sure, whites institutionalize their love for whiteness in their social systems, institutions, and community organizations. If you are white and you are willing to play by the rules, you will be taken care of. Logical thinking rather than emotional thinking is the key to success. Learning to think with the logic of one's own mind rather than emotions is the quickest way to achieve life goals.

10. EMBRACING A SPIRIT OF VOLUNTEERISM

A spirit of volunteerism is a salient value in American culture. Volunteerism helps individuals to become cause oriented. Volunteering to assist those less fortunate than you are can put your own worries in perspective. The more you pay attention to the needs of others, the easier it is to forget about your own anxieties in life.

CONCLUSION

Human values define how individuals view the world and their place in the scheme of things. Values are the social basis for institutional arrangements, social processes, and above all lifestyles. To be sure then values are priorities. Values are reflections of where individuals place their ultimate trust. Identify an individual's treasure, and there you will find his heart. In short, values dictate mindset and worldview.

Without a doubt, the American capitalistic value system is an external materialistic view of the world which in effect is grounded in the notion of the survival of the fittest. Thus, in American society the worth of the individual is solely determined by material possessions. In other words, capitalism does not value the human personality in and of itself. Materialism as a way of life adversely affects human personality structure as well as human interaction. But, more importantly, materialism creates a static system of logic rather than a dynamic system of organizing how one comes to know, or one's understanding.

In devaluing selfhood, individuals participate in non-being—that is, they deny the spiritual ground of their own existence. Material values create violence as well as societal disorganization. Valuing material goodies in and of themselves creates despair in terms of intellectual integrity and moral character. Hence, materialism as a way of life fosters social contradictions rather than ethical consistency.

Our external materialistic value orientation creates artificial and arbitrary scarcities. But, more importantly, materialism engenders a negative individualistic ethos rather than human interdependence. Materialism as a way of life has caused Americans to institutionalize selfish hoarding rather than human interdependence as the foundation of human interaction. Modern mentality then is grounded in greed, envy, and jealousy. Because of this social fact, humankind is in fact the endangered species. Indeed, we have institutionalized specific social processes that have placed humankind in conflict with itself (self-estrangement), natural laws, and above all social groupings different in kind from one's own. We need to find the universal dimension, the unifying force, in our differences. Difference in the human community simply means difference, not inequity or inequality. In fact, our differences are the source of our strength, both internally as well as externally. A multiethnic and multiracial society cannot afford the luxury of playing up social differences in negative ways. It is for this reason alone that American society is becoming increasingly more chaotic.

Even the value orientation of institutional religion is too materialistic. Indeed, the individualistic-materialistic value orientation of institutional religion renders it irrelevant. Religion ought to be about intangibles rather than materialism. In fact, institutional religion has no "focused ought." Religion then ought to foster "moral order" and therefore enhance social cohesion in society rather than conflict. Instead, institutional religion has become the main vehicle for advancing racism, sexism, individualism, and above all authoritarianism.

In each essay the reader has been confronted with the values problem, which in effect is a question about the meaning of individual existence in society. The question is, how do we learn to live together in human societies without destroying one another? War and street violence is not the answer. We must give peace a chance. In short, the problem of individual existence in society is essentially a problem of spiritual meaning.

Therefore, the greatest threat to the survival of American society is not posed by external ideologies and foreign military regimes, but rather by our own materialistic value orientation, which in part is the basis for our social disorganization politically and economically, as well as the institutionalization of greed. For those who lived through the Cold War period of the 1980s, the Russians are not coming; they have arrived. In fact, they have been here for quite some time. The Russian mentality came over on the Mayflower: rule of the few over the many. It is indeed our value orientation and "either/or" logical thought processes that have us in the horrible mess we are in. Rather than roads, railways, and bridges, moral values and intellectual integrity must form the foundation of a democratic society's infrastructure.